BECOMING TALENTED

A SYSTEMATIC METHOD FOR THE DEVELOPMENT OF EAR TRAINING AND MUSIC READING SKILLS

ISADOR MILLER

MUSICAL SKILLS PRESS

CONTENTS

Acknowledgments   ix

Who Is This Book For?   xi

Introduction   xv

PART ONE
THEORY

1. SKILL DEVELOPMENT AND TALENT   3

Early Learning and the Critical Period   4

Absolute Pitch   7

Accessibility   7

Setting Up the System   8

Aural Skills and Synthesis   10

The Three Fundamental Skills   11

Fundamental vs. Advanced Skills   11

Prerequisite Knowledge   12

Language, Music, and Complexity   13

Rules, Grammar, and Fluency   14

Conscious Thought   16

2. FUNDAMENTAL SKILL #1: KEYBOARD
VISUALIZATION   18

Mental Practice   20

Intervallic Reading and Clefs   20

Analogies   22

3. FUNDAMENTAL SKILL #2: REAL-TIME MUSIC
READING   25

Vocalization and Understanding   26

Solfège Syllables   26

Fixed-Do vs. Moveable-Do   28

4. FUNDAMENTAL SKILL #3: AURAL
   IDENTIFICATION   30
   All Identification Is Intervallic   31
   Vertical vs. Horizontal Intervals   33
   Reference Points   34

5. COMBINING ALL THREE SKILLS   36

PART TWO
PRACTICE

6. PRACTICE OVERVIEW   41

7. FUNDAMENTAL SKILL #1: KEYBOARD
   VISUALIZATION   44
   Using the Hand   45
   The Nature of the Visualization   45
   Solfège Syllables, Preparatory Exercise: Naming
   Individual Pitches   46
   Intervals   47

8. KEYBOARD VISUALIZATION EXERCISES,
   SOLFÈGE SYLLABLES   50
   1.1) Individual Pitch Naming/Visualization   50
   1.2) White-Key Interval Cycles   51
   1.3) Directed White-Key Tracking   52
   1.4) Random Number Generator White-Key Tracking   54
   1.5) Tracking Line Interval Identification   55
   1.6) White-Key Tracking, Solfège Syllables   58
   1.7) 15-Line Tracking, Solfège Syllables   60
   1.8) White-Key 7-Note Row   63

9. HALF-STEP INTERVAL (HSI) IDENTIFICATION   66
   1.9) HSI Cycles   69
   1.10) Directed HSI Tracking   70
   1.11) Random Number Generator HSI Tracking   70
   1.12) Vertical HSI Tracking, Spoken   71
   1.13) Horizontal HSI Tracking, Spoken   72
   1.14) Full Tracking Protocol, Spoken   73
   1.15) HSI 7-Note Row   74
   1.16) HSI 21-Note Row   75

10. SCALE/CHORD VISUALIZATION 77

    1.17) Basic Scale Visualization 78

    1.18) Tracking Lines in Key 78

    1.19) Chord Visualization 79

    1.20) Keyboard Improvisation 80

11. FUNDAMENTAL SKILL #2: REAL-TIME MUSIC
    READING 81

12. RHYTHM READING 83

    Beats and Subdivisions 83

    Understanding Rhythm Notation 85

13. VOCALIZED FEATURE STACKING 89

    2.1) Rhythm 91

    2.2) Solfège Syllables 92

    2.3) Scale Degrees 93

    2.4) Vertical HSIs 94

    2.5) Horizontal HSIs 95

    2.6) Jazz/Pop Chords 96

    2.7) Miscellaneous Features 97

    Vocalization Challenges 97

14. POLYPHONIC MUSIC READING 99

    2.8) Polyphonic Solfège/HSI Vocalization 99

    2.9) Advanced Keyboard Improvisation 104

    2.10) Keyboard Sight Reading 105

15. FUNDAMENTAL SKILL #3: AURAL
    IDENTIFICATION 109

    3.1) Vertical Identification Over a Drone 111

    3.2) Ploger Interval Drills, Harmonic Intervals 113

    3.3) Interval Drills, Melodic Intervals 117

    3.4) Interval Drills, Three or More Notes 118

    3.5) Vertical Improvisation Over a Drone 119

    3.6) Horizontal Improvisation 120

    3.7) Melodic Improvisation 121

    3.8) Accompanied Improvisation 122

    3.9) Random Number Generator HSI Singing 122

    3.10) Vertical HSI Tracking, Sung 123

    3.11) Horizontal HSI Tracking, Sung 123

3.12) Scale Visualization, Sung   124

3.13) Scale Context Transformation   124

3.14) Single-Note Context Creation   127

3.15) Arpeggio Singing   128

3.16) Interval Comparison   131

3.17) Full Tracking Protocol, Spoken and Sung   131

3.18) 21-Note Row, Sung   132

A Note on Intonation   132

16. SYNTHESIS   134

17. SYNTHESIS: SIGHT SINGING   136

A) Singing Using Solfège Syllables   136

B) Isolating Problems Using the Feature Stacking
Protocol   137

C) Feature Stacking, Sung   137

Feature Flexibility   139

18. SYNTHESIS: DICTATION   141

A) Input Phase   142

B) Identification Phase   143

C) Writing Phase   145

Harmonic Dictation   146

Input and Identification Practice   147

Debugging   147

19. FINAL THOUGHTS: MOTIVATION, PROGRESS,
AND TALENT   148

20. APPENDIX A: CLEF REFERENCE   150

21. APPENDIX B: MAJOR AND MINOR SCALES/KEYS   151

22. APPENDIX C: CHORDS   155

23. APPENDIX D: TRANSPOSITION   158

A) The Transposition Process   159

B) Transposing Instruments   160

C) Accidentals   163

24. APPENDIX E: EXERCISE REFERENCE   164

Fundamental Skill #1: Keyboard Visualization   164

Fundamental Skill #2: Real-Time Music Reading   167

Fundamental Skill #3: Aural Identification   168

Synthesis: Sight Singing   171
Synthesis: Dictation   171

25. GLOSSARY   173

Bibliography and Exercise Compilations   175
About the Author   177

ACKNOWLEDGMENTS

This book would not have been possible without the influence of Marianne Ploger, whose ideas and instruction enormously impacted how I conceive of the music learning process, especially regarding keyboard visualization and the importance of understanding interval sounds and relationships.

I would also like to thank Dr. Lindsey Reymore, who helped me train my own musicianship abilities and was tremendously supportive, encouraging, and generous with her time and attention. Her mentorship was indispensable, and many of the ideas in this book are the result of her guidance.

I also want to express my gratitude to Cristy Kouri, Drew Gatlin, and any other friends and colleagues who provided editorial assistance with this project. Additionally, I must thank my current and former students, who enabled me to refine this method in the "real world."

Finally, I would like to thank my wife, Tina, whose endless patience, encouragement, and support were indispensable when writing, editing, and re-editing this book. The publication of this book, as well as most other good things in my life, would be unimaginable without her.

WHO IS THIS BOOK FOR?

Becoming Talented offers a systematic and reliable method to acquire musical talent. This method is effective for anyone with any level of musical experience, whether you are a complete beginner or a professional musician with years of experience. The terminology and exercises in this book may seem unusual if you have some musical experience, but do not let that dissuade you; this method is crafted to maximally improve your ability to play, write, and understand music. Almost all the exercises are performed in your mind rather than on an instrument, and these exercises will powerfully reshape your entire conception of music, enhancing your musical abilities. Contrary to popular opinion, your level of musical talent is not a fixed gift from nature; with the proper strategies, it can be enormously improved.

This method does not contain a "quick fix" or "a few simple tricks" for improving your musical ability; instead, it offers a targeted approach to completely restructure the way you think about music. Because this method is designed to produce extensive improvements as efficiently as possible, the exercises in this book will be very challenging and mentally strenuous; they will push you out of your comfort zone and require focus and perseverance. The good news is that incredible gains can appear quite swiftly. It is not easy to give a precise timeline for progress.

If you consistently practice the exercises in this book, you should notice a significant advancement in your musical fluency within two or three months. With six months to a year of diligent practice, you will undoubtedly experience profound improvement in your musical abilities. Even more remarkable, these newfound abilities will feel natural and easy, empowering you to perform challenging musical feats that may have previously seemed impossible.

This book is not a typical ear training, aural skills, or music-reading manual. Most resources on these subjects merely contain increasingly difficult musical excerpts to play or sing, presuming that the reader will somehow get better at these tasks with enough practice. These resources may contain a few pages of helpful hints, but unfortunately, they tell the reader almost nothing about *how* to perform the included exercises; nothing is said about what your thought process should be, how to address specific weaknesses, or what to do if repeated practice does not work. This book is different. In this method, you will find explicit instructions that will walk you through the process of improving your understanding of musical sound and notation; this book describes how to improve your musical abilities and how to direct your thought process while performing musical tasks.

You will need the following very basic materials to work through this method: music staff paper, a pen/pencil, and some sort of rudimentary keyboard instrument. The keyboard instrument could be a full-size piano, but even a small toy keyboard or a piano keyboard app on a smartphone, tablet, or computer is perfectly sufficient. You do not need a full-size instrument of any kind to work through the exercises in this book; you only need a device that can generate the sounds of specific notes.

The exercises in this book do not cater to a specific instrumental background; although pianists may have a slight advantage, this method is effective regardless of your primary instrument and is even effective for singers who do not play any instruments. This method does not discriminate based on musical style/genre—it is equally helpful whether you play classical music, popular music, jazz, R&B, funk, metal, etc. It is similarly applicable whether you are (or would like to be) a performer, composer, arranger, producer, pop songwriter, etc.

You may find this method especially helpful if you have a significant amount of textbook knowledge or instrumental ability but have always struggled with music reading or ear training, or if you are highly motivated but have always considered yourself untalented. In such cases, you may experience exceptionally rapid improvement. Remember that this method does not just improve your musical ability—it will enable you to **become talented**.

This method would also be valuable for educators, specifically instructors of high school or college-level aural skills or music theory courses. The exercises in this book can be adapted and simplified to accommodate students of any age or level of experience and can even be practical for elementary school music students. This book would be excellent if used in its totality as a textbook for an aural skills curriculum, or exercises may be strategically selected to fit within a structured curriculum.

This method may *not* be for you if you have no musical experience and your goals do not include musical fluency. If your goal is learning to play several of your favorite songs on an instrument, this book *can* help you achieve that goal, but this method is very intensive and may not be the quickest route to learn a few easy songs; any other instructional method may be more practical for very modest musical goals. However, if you are highly motivated and want to bring your musical abilities to an exceptionally high level, this book is perfect for you. You can achieve incredible results with this method even if you are a complete novice with zero musical experience, but it will require a great deal of effort and dedication.

Here, I present a list of skills/abilities that practicing the method in this book can help facilitate. This list is not exhaustive, but it is presented to make clear the specific practical abilities you can develop to incredible heights by working through this method:

1. Improved sight reading.
2. More fluent improvisation.
3. Easier memorization of music.
4. Fluent sight singing.

5. Rapidly learning pieces of music by ear and easily transcribing them as music notation.

6. Easily transposing notated or memorized music into other keys.

7. Playing and/or singing back a musical passage after a single listening.

8. Writing/composing music directly onto a score or into music production software, knowing what it will sound like without the need to play/hear it first.

9. More creative freedom when composing music.

10. Arranging music of all genres, including (but not limited to) classical, jazz, pop, metal, and hip-hop.

11. Playing pieces of music by ear from memory, totally unprepared, i.e., immediately playing pieces you have heard before, never having studied them or spent any time actively learning how to play them.

12. Looking at musical scores, even large orchestral scores, and hearing them in your head.

13. Playing keyboard versions of large multi-instrument musical scores upon first seeing the score, also called playing a "keyboard reduction."

14. A deeper understanding of diverse musical styles, allowing you to easily mimic the style of your favorite composer, songwriter, arranger, improviser, etc.

15. The ability to step into a live musical ensemble and play with minimal or no preparation.

16. Improved rhythmic accuracy, i.e., playing more "in the pocket."

17. Improved sense of pitch and intonation.

18. Greater appreciation for unfamiliar or complex musical styles.

19. More efficient practice sessions.

20. Increased musicality in your performances.

INTRODUCTION

I was highly driven and hardworking when I first began playing music at the age of thirteen; however, I routinely encountered other musicians who worked much less hard yet seemed more capable. I had assumed that many hours of practice and study would compensate for what I assumed was my lack of natural musical talent. Extensive practice worked up to a point—I was highly knowledgeable and quite technically proficient, teaching music and working as a gigging musician throughout my twenties. Maintaining a high level of musicianship was arduous work, and it required many hours of technical exercises and repetitive mechanical practice that other seemingly more talented musicians did not appear to require.

Despite all this practice, my music reading ability was mediocre. I was also unable to hear and identify musical elements that other musicians could easily hear and identify; this discrepancy was especially wide when I compared myself to those who began musical training as very young children. No matter what I did or how much I practiced, my ability to hear and identify musical sounds (often called "ear training" or "aural skills") barely improved. When I encountered musicians whose music reading or aural acuity greatly exceeded my own, they could not tell me how they developed these abilities and rarely had any insight regarding how they performed seemingly superhuman musical feats. Most of these musicians did not seem exceptionally gifted in areas other than music, which seemed strange considering their staggering musical abilities. This incongruity led me to conclude that rather than being more intelligent, knowledgeable, or harder working than myself, these musicians must be using a cognitive process different from my own to understand and interact with music. If I could figure out how these cognitive systems operated, I could retrain the mind to engage in music more like these talented musicians, resulting in the acquisition of musical talent.

I did not believe that starting musical training at a very young age was necessary to become a great musician, and I thought there must be some way to acquire the abilities that seem so natural in musicians who started training in early childhood. Fortunately, I discovered the methods of Marianne Ploger, who was the director of the musicianship program at Vanderbilt University and a former student of renowned pedagogue Nadia Boulanger, teacher of hundreds of the twentieth century's most prominent musicians, such as composer Aaron Copland, composer/producer Quincy Jones (who famously produced three of Michael Jackson's most successful albums), minimalist composer Philip Glass, songwriter Burt Bacharach, and tango composer Astor Piazzolla, just to name a few.

Marianne Ploger developed strategies that could help any musician improve, regardless of their ostensible level of natural talent. Rather than offering the typical advice of just practicing more, her method focused on making considerable changes to how students conceptualize music, filling in cognitive gaps and enabling musicians to complete challenging musical tasks with relative ease. I studied Marianne Ploger's method for a few years, which changed my entire approach to musical skill acquisition and led to a massive increase in my musical abilities.

Using my experiences with Marianne Ploger as a springboard, I spent the following years studying historical methodologies for teaching music, applying cognitive science research, and using empirical experience with my own students to craft a method that can systematically help any musician of any age or ability level acquire the skills that are often associated with musical talent. This method has allowed me to effortlessly perform musical tasks that had previously felt impossible. I have also taught many students of all ages using this method, enabling students with no prior musical experience to comfortably perform impressive musical feats within a few months—feats that even musicians with decades of experience often struggle with.

I have compiled this method into this book. I do not present hard scientific evidence for the efficacy of this method because I do not believe there are currently any scientific studies that could categorically validate it. While many findings in modern cognitive science are consistent with strategies outlined in this book, I believe this method stands on its own based on its practical efficacy rather than a theoretical justification drawn from scientific studies.

I describe the method and rational support for its efficacy in the **Theory** section at the beginning of this book. I also discuss the ideas of talent and skill and why I disagree with prominent narratives regarding musical talent. I then introduce the three fundamental skills essential for musical fluency that this method will help you develop.

Following the **Theory** section is the **Practice** section, which describes exercises for developing the three fundamental skills and explains how to combine these three skills for practical use. You do not need to practice these exercises in strict order, but I have ordered the exercises for each fundamental skill so that they will generally build on abilities acquired from prior exercises for that skill. You should strive to achieve fluency in every exercise, but practicing any exercise to any extent will help improve your musical abilities. If you find a specific exercise to be particularly difficult, that means the mental process it targets is not sufficiently developed, so the more challenging an exercise is, the more time and attention you should devote to it. Even exercises that initially seem easy should be attempted at progressively faster speeds when applicable. Practicing the exercises will significantly improve your musical abilities; you only need dedication and determination. The process will not be easy, but with continued practice, you will feel yourself **becoming talented**.

PART ONE
THEORY

Skill Development and Talent

Musical talent does not depend on innate ability but rather on a constellation of interconnected skills that emerge from a musician's cognitive process for interacting with music. Every musician develops a set of personal cognitive processes for engaging with music, and most musicians develop these processes unconsciously. If a music student instinctively constructs a cognitive system that is highly efficient for processing music, that student will generally excel and be labeled as musically talented or as having "good ears." Students who develop these efficient cognitive systems at an early age are completely unaware that they are using any specific system at all. These musicians are often entirely unable to explain how they perform challenging musical tasks; that is, they "can just do it." Some of these musicians go on to teach music with questionable success. Because they are unaware of how they developed their own abilities, it is often very difficult for them to bring about significant advancements in their students' abilities.

When performing challenging musical tasks, a musician who has unconsciously developed some of the cognitive tools necessary to perform such tasks may gradually improve. Unfortunately, many of these musicians reach a point at which their naturally acquired abilities are insufficient for increasingly challenging material, and they lack any reliable way to improve the cognitive tools through which these abilities operate. Even more unfortunate, musicians who have not developed *any* of the cognitive tools required to perform challenging musical tasks will be completely unable to perform such tasks and will barely improve with any amount of practice. These musicians may spend a great deal of time practicing, but most practice methods do not directly address the cognitive tools that these musicians lack. Sadly, these students often think of themselves as musically untalented. What most people call "musical talent" is merely the presence of an efficient cognitive system through which the musician conceives of musical sound and notation, facilitating the capacity to perform challenging musical tasks with ease.

Fortunately, with the proper strategies and exercises, you can build a highly efficient cognitive system for processing music. Such a system relies on specific fundamental cognitive skills which can be acquired and developed. Anyone can acquire and develop these skills to radically improve their musical fluency. Musical talent arises from an efficient cognitive system for processing music; because working with the exercises in this book can help build and develop such a system, these exercises can increase your level of musical talent.

EARLY LEARNING AND THE CRITICAL PERIOD

There is a widely held assumption that a high level of musical ability is only attainable for those who begin musical training in early childhood, specifically at or before the age of five or six, and those who start training later can never acquire exceptional musical fluency. Though this assumption is statistically well-founded, it suggests a direct causal relationship between early childhood training and musical ability that is not necessarily justified. There is undoubtedly a correlation between early musical training and later success in music, but this relationship is not as directly causal as commonly believed.

There is a concept in language acquisition known as the "critical period," a period in which a child must have exposure to language, otherwise the child will never be able to speak or understand any language. Many musicians and music teachers believe there is a similar critical period in music, and a child will only develop high-level musical abilities if training begins at an early age. This critical period in music training is typically thought to be physiological. Many presume that children's brains are biologically capable of processes that adult brains are incapable of, resulting in easier acquisition of musical abilities for children. Indeed, most great adult musicians did begin musical training at a very young age; however, this correlation is not the result of neurological limits affected by biological age; instead, it emerges from differences between children's and adults' cognitive and behavioral learning strategies.

Adult music learners typically engage in music learning through cognitive strategies they have developed for other purposes; for instance, adult learners will try to perform music tasks with cognitive strategies they had developed for solving mathematical problems, analyzing data, practicing purely physical coordinative tasks, etc. These adult learners are not saying to themselves, "I am going to play a piece of music using a cognitive strategy I developed for data analysis," but they will instinctively use the cognitive strategies that are available to them, strategies that had been highly effective for these other purposes. While these strategies may feel secure and reliable because of their familiarity and effectiveness in other domains, they are rarely effective for engaging in music because they were constructed to perform different tasks. In contrast, children intuitively create cognitive strategies specifically *for* processing music; children do not process music through cognitive strategies created for other purposes because such musically inefficient strategies have yet to be established and ingrained.

Compared to children, adults are very intellectually proficient. Adults can use complex linguistic forms, comprehend complicated systems, and understand logic much better than children—so why would an adult have a more difficult time acquiring musical ability? One problem with adult music learners *is* that they are so much more intellectually capable. Because of this, the adult music learner never engages with the fundamental cognitive abilities required to understand music. Most adults completely skip the most basic listening skills necessary for musical fluency and are unaware that they are doing so. Adults will create complex rules, mnemonic devices, and rigorous repetitive mechanical practice methods to learn music; unfortunately, this is often done without any understanding of musical sounds. Adults are so concerned with performance outcomes that they rarely open themselves up to hearing and mastering the rudimentary perceptual elements of music. In contrast, when children learn music, they are focused primarily on understanding musical sounds and care little about accelerated performance outcomes.

Children's physical abilities are also very undeveloped compared to adults, so many children will develop their understanding of musical sounds in conjunction with their ability to perform music on an instrument. Adults have highly developed physical coordination skills, and they often immediately try to play challenging pieces of music without understanding what the music should sound like, rarely experiencing an aural understanding of what they are playing. The effects of this can be seen in many adult beginner pianists when trying to play pieces with both hands. These pianists often struggle mightily with two-hand playing—not because their hands are less physically capable than children's hands, but because they are trying to play multiple simultaneous streams of music before they can *understand* multiple simultaneous streams of music. Because adult music learners routinely engage in a strictly physical method of playing, even when one of these adult pianists manages to force their way through a piece requiring both hands, usually through sheer mechanical repetition, the results often sound unmusical, robotic, and strictly mechanical; this is no surprise because without understanding the sounds of the music, the resultant performance *is* strictly mechanical.

This book presents a straightforward method of circumventing the challenges adult learners face, facilitating the acquisition of a robust understanding of musical sound and notation for learners of any age. The cognitive strategies acquired through the exercises in this book resemble the strategies that some young learners acquire intuitively. Not all children are lucky enough to intuitively develop optimal cognitive systems for processing music; therefore, the exercises in this book are equally helpful for enhancing young learners' musical skills and talents.

ABSOLUTE PITCH

One potential exception to my skepticism of a musical critical period is the ability known as **absolute pitch**, also called **perfect pitch**. This term refers to the ability of a musician to hear one or more notes totally out of context and immediately identify what specific note(s) they heard. Almost universally, children only seem to acquire this ability when they start musical training around the age of five or earlier. While it may be possible to develop absolute pitch ability as an adult learner, there does not yet seem to be a reliable way to do so, and there is some evidence that this ability may have a genetic component.

The strategies in this book will help musicians achieve fluency with relative pitch, i.e., the sounds of the relationships between notes, and through these methods, it is possible to gain abilities that are practically indistinguishable from those of a musician with absolute pitch. The exercises in this book may help you develop a rough sense of absolute pitch, but that is not the primary intent of this method. Importantly, those who possess absolute pitch are not always superior musicians. Because almost all music listeners do *not* have absolute pitch, a musician lacking this ability is better positioned to understand the listening experiences of most music audiences. Some musicians with absolute pitch do not have any sense of relative pitch. If you are a musician with absolute pitch, you will be happy to learn that the strategies in this book can help you better understand relative pitch, thus playing or composing more musically and understanding music more deeply.

An in-depth discussion of absolute pitch is beyond the scope of this book, but I offer some words of encouragement: you do **not** need to possess absolute pitch to have extremely well-developed aural abilities. Many musicians who lack absolute pitch far outperform musicians who have absolute pitch. Do not become discouraged if you do not have absolute pitch.

ACCESSIBILITY

Traditionally, substantial musical training could only be achieved by musicians from families with the financial means to pay for expensive instruments and years of music lessons for their children. Many families cannot afford these luxuries, and many potential music students may not have a safe place to keep an expensive instrument even if they could afford one. Fortunately, the method contained in this book requires very little financial investment and can be practiced without any costly equipment. A rudimentary piano keyboard is necessary, but even an inexpensive toy keyboard or digital piano/keyboard app on a phone, tablet, or computer can suffice; if none of these are available, any instrument or device that can generate musical tones can be used instead of a keyboard. The method outlined in this book provides a way to develop musical talent for those who might not otherwise have the opportunity. Because this method does not mandate rigorous and expensive early childhood training, it enables those from diverse backgrounds to fully develop their musical abilities. Musicians need not have their musical potential held hostage by the financial circumstances of their childhood.

SETTING UP THE SYSTEM

This book does not present a few helpful hints and quick tips for improving musical ability. Instead, it presents a method to completely recreate your process for understanding music. This method can totally restructure the cognitive framework you use to engage with music, and if you follow the strategies in this book, you will hear and understand music in an entirely new way. Restructuring your cognitive process for understanding music can initially be very uncomfortable and frustrating. Sometimes, it will feel like you have made significant progress, but you may feel like you cannot successfully perform any exercises the next day. Do not worry about this; you will make considerable progress over time if you continue practicing.

It might be helpful to think of your musical ability as being controlled by a "mental music device," an apparatus in your mind that you use to understand music. This book will help you improve this device, but the process may not feel as direct as you would like; there will be large fluctuations in your musical ability as you develop your mental music device. By analogy, imagine repairing the hardware in a computer. To perform such a repair, you would have to disassemble the computer, repair or add/remove certain parts, and then reassemble it again to use it; however, when you have disassembled the computer and are in the process of repairing it, the computer is inoperable. Following the strategies in this book can be considered a process of disassembling, repairing, and reassembling your mental music device. Performing the exercises in this book may be thought of as the disassembly and repair stages—your mind will take care of the reassembling stage on its own over time. There may be times when you have disassembled your mental music device and made significant repairs, but it may take a day or two for your mind to reassemble it so that it works again. During these times, do not be afraid to hold off on practicing for a few days and see how everything feels afterward. Because you will be making such profound changes to the way you think about music, it may take some time before you can make practical use of these changes.

Once your mental music device is sufficiently assembled and functional, you will helplessly filter all musical tasks through this device, and it will gradually improve on its own if you regularly interact with music. Remember that your mental music device can become increasingly efficient; even if your musical abilities seem to be improving without much effort, the targeted practice of challenging exercises is still valuable.

Practice is necessary, but the right kind of practice filtered through an efficient cognitive system is essential to improve your skills. So-called "naturally talented" musicians often spend significant time practicing because practice is enjoyable for them, as they have a cognitive system that efficiently processes music. It often appears that musicians who spend more time practicing become better, and of course, this is generally true. However, many musicians with inefficient cognitive tools for understanding music will practice for countless hours with little musical ability to show for it. The *Becoming Talented* exercises hone your cognitive tools for processing music and will improve any task that uses these tools. Through this process, practice will become more rewarding, productive, and enjoyable, leading to more efficient and less frustrating practice sessions. Not only will this lead to better results from your practice, but it will likely inspire you to spend more time practicing because practicing will be less repetitive and feel less tedious.

AURAL SKILLS AND SYNTHESIS

The tasks that best display high levels of musical ability are often called **aural skills**. The prototypical aural skills tasks are sight-singing and dictation. Sight singing is the act of looking at a notated piece of music, generally a melody, and singing it out loud with no prior preparation. Dictation, also known as transcription, involves listening to a passage of music and transcribing the notes and rhythms using music notation. The ability to perform these aural skills tasks reflects a musician's capacity to understand music deeply and fluently.

Both sight-singing and dictation are high-level abilities that rely on synthesizing multiple lower-level skills. The ability to perform sight-singing and dictation tasks arises from the development of multiple skills that work together to enable you to perform these tasks. You can think of sight-singing and dictation as tests of your ability to imagine, identify, and label musical sounds. Sight-singing and dictation tasks are the most straightforward ways to verify the development of these abilities.

Unless a musician is a singer, the act of sight singing may not seem practically useful in and of itself; however, sight singing is beneficial because it engages the musician's capacity to understand what music sounds like just from looking at the notation, much like how fluent readers of written language can look at that language's writing and "hear it" in their head. The ability to imagine music in your mind is known as **audiation**, which is central to musical fluency. Many musicians think of music notation as a guide for what to do with their hands on an instrument; however, the best musicians understand that music notation also tells you how the music *sounds*. Audiation is a valuable ability even if you are not ultimately concerned with reading music notation; hearing musical sounds in your mind is just as useful for improvisation and musical traditions that do not use Western music notation.

Dictation tasks may seem similarly impractical—rarely will a musician need to write down music upon first hearing it; however, like sight singing, dictation is more about the underlying abilities it exhibits rather than the practical utility of the task itself. Dictation tasks demonstrate the musician's ability to recognize and label musical sounds and rela-tionships. The act of notating music is less important than the level of musical understanding demonstrated by the ability to identify and label what you are hearing in the music. For example, many skilled jazz musi-cians can listen to a melody and immediately play it back on their instru-ment without having the ability or need to notate the melody on paper.

The Three Fundamental Skills

The three fundamental skills that can be developed through the exer-cises in this book are:

1. **Keyboard Visualization**
2. **Real-Time Music Reading**
3. **Aural Identification**

Developing these three fundamental skills will build and improve your cognitive system for understanding music, allowing you to interact fluently with music of any genre. Some musicians may have substan-tially developed one or two of these skills unconsciously. However, most musicians will have significant weaknesses in all three skills. There is considerable overlap between the Keyboard Visualization skill and the Real-Time Music Reading skill, and any development of these skills should benefit the Aural Identification skill. That said, you must indi-vidually target and develop all three skills to achieve high levels of musical fluency.

Fundamental vs. Advanced Skills

While the exercises in this book may seem challenging, the skills and abilities developed through these exercises are not advanced musical skills; they are genuine music fundamentals, the basis upon which you should build all your musical abilities. Many of the exercises in this book may seem unusual, but this is intentional—the exercises are carefully constructed so that they deliberately circumvent inefficient cognitive processes for understanding music, forcing you to engage in new and more efficient ways of conceptualizing musical sound and notation. These exercises will force you to learn music like a child, bypassing the complex and inefficient cognitive strategies adults tend to engage in when practicing music.

Though some exercises in this book may feel incredibly challenging, you should resist the urge to avoid an exercise just because it is difficult. Do not tell yourself that you are not ready for these exercises yet, regardless of your prior level of musical experience. Many of these exercises are just as tricky for musicians with decades of experience as they are for complete beginners. Because these exercises develop fundamental musical skills, no prior experience is needed to practice them, but remember that this does not mean these exercises will be easy.

PREREQUISITE KNOWLEDGE

Very little prerequisite knowledge is required to practice this method, and most of the exercises herein require no prior musical training. Some exercises require knowledge of major and minor scales and the sharps/flats in each key; Appendix B contains a brief discussion of scale construction and a chart showing all major and minor keys. You can still make significant progress even if you totally skip the exercises that require an understanding of major/minor scales.

A basic understanding of rhythm notation (quarter notes, half notes, etc.), meter, and time signatures in music is necessary to develop Fundamental Skill #2: Real-Time Music Reading. This knowledge should be available in any resource that explains music or rhythm fundamentals, and the Fundamental Skill #2 section explains the basics of meter and how to understand and accurately reproduce any rhythm. For some musicians, a knowledge of chords and Roman numeral notation will be helpful; Appendix C contains a brief overview of this information. If you do not have sufficient knowledge in one of these areas, feel free to continue working through any of the other exercises in this book while learning about these topics from other sources. You need not have any prior knowledge of music theory to derive great benefit from these exercises. Improving your performance of any exercise in this book will significantly enhance your musicianship, and this method works to whatever extent you engage with it, whether you pick and choose some exercises or extensively practice all of them. Of course, eventually working through every exercise will help you derive maximum benefit from this method, but you should work through exercises at whatever pace and level of engagement is sustainable for you.

LANGUAGE, MUSIC, AND COMPLEXITY

When children acquire language, they do not immediately produce and understand complex sentences. Children first acquire an understanding of the sounds of a language, followed by basic nouns and verbs, and gradually produce increasingly complex phrases. Unfortunately, many adult musicians try to produce and understand complex musical phrases without understanding the basic sounds and structures of music. For example, an adult musician may attempt to transcribe a complicated melody by ear before they can contextually identify a single note by ear. This transcription task quickly becomes tedious and often turns into a "guess and check" process, where little actual aural identification occurs.

Similarly, an adult musician may try to sight-sing a complex melody without being able to identify intervals contained in the melody and without knowing what those intervals sound like, resulting in much frustration and failure. Many of these adult musicians are highly motivated; they may practice sight-singing or transcribing music for hours but have little to show for it and barely improve. To form a linguistic analogy, these musicians are trying to produce and understand complex sentences before they understand the basic sounds of the language. Failure in a sight-singing or dictation/transcription task is almost always the result of a shortcoming in one of the three fundamental skills. Breaking down the practice process into the three fundamental skills described in this book will allow you to directly develop the essential abilities that struggling musicians often lack. While these skills are fundamental, they are not easy to acquire—the exercises for developing these skills may feel highly challenging despite their apparent simplicity.

RULES, GRAMMAR, AND FLUENCY

Many highly intellectually capable musicians develop complex systems of rules to assist in their playing, composing, or improvising. Examples of these rules are those used in writing counterpoint and four-part harmony, constructing chord progressions, understanding form in composition, using specific scales/modes for improvisation, etc. These rules are often bewilderingly complex and use arcane music theory terminology; musicians prone to methodical thinking will spend many hours memorizing these rules and dogmatically abiding by them. An example of one of these rules for a jazz musician might be something like "Over a dominant seventh chord, you can play the melodic minor scale with a tonic a perfect fifth above the root of the dominant seventh chord." A classical composer might be taught to use a rule such as "Construct a melody in period form by ending the first four measures with a half cadence with the melody on scale-degree two; follow this by four measures beginning the same way as the initial four measures but ending in a perfect authentic cadence with a tonic in the melody."

Most of these rules are the result of music theoretic analyses of the compositions or performances of great musicians, and it is often assumed that the great musicians whose music was analyzed to discover these rules were consciously thinking about these specific rules to create their music. An observed musical outcome is not necessarily the result of the musician consciously and intentionally striving to achieve that outcome in the same terms through which the outcome was observed and described. Put another way, studying the grammar of music does not necessarily tell you anything about how musical forms were arrived at by the creators of these forms. This circumstance can be highly misleading, as even musicians who are not consciously following these rules might describe them in such terms. A skilled jazz musician with a significant knowledge of music theory might describe an improvised passage they had played using highly technical music theory jargon: "I played a B diminished seventh arpeggio over the rhythm section's G7 to imply a G7 ♭ 9 chord, emphasizing the resolution to the following C minor chord." While this might be the most precise way to describe such a passage from a music theoretic standpoint, such descriptions are often post hoc rationalizations of resultant structures; they are descriptions of musical structures rather than descriptions of the thought processes used to create those structures. In other words, these rules are derived from what musicians are *doing*, not necessarily what they are *thinking*.

To demonstrate this point, speak any simple sentence; for example, "I am reading a book about music right now." Any native English speaker, even a young child, has absolutely no problem producing or understanding such a sentence. Now ask yourself: how did you produce this utterance? Do you know what "rules" you used to create this sentence? Why did you say "right now" at the end of the phrase rather than somewhere in the middle? You could have said, "I am right now reading a book about music." Though not incomprehensible, this might sound a bit strange to most English speakers. Compare that slightly strange sentence to "I am currently reading a book about music." This similar sentence sounds better, but do you know why? And if you do not know why, does this stop you from producing and understanding such a sentence with the utmost ease?

We could look at our example sentence and tell ourselves a story about how we created it, labeling each word's part of speech and analyzing its grammatical function. We used a pronoun, an auxiliary verb, present progressive tense, etc. Such an analysis might be interesting, and we might even be tempted to say it explains how we produced the sentence; however, consider the final words: "right now." Most native English speakers would have to think very hard to identify what part of speech these two words are in this context, making it unlikely that any conscious grammatical rules were followed to construct this sentence. Taking this point further, turn the same sentence into a question: "Am I reading a book about music right now?" This change in construction is effortless (although after the prior two paragraphs, you may no longer be sure of the answer to this question). You might look at this question and observe that a "rule" would state that you should switch the order of the pronoun and auxiliary verb to achieve this interrogative form; however, you almost certainly had no conscious conception of this rule; this construction just "sounds right."

Like our example sentence in English, a musician may invoke ostensible grammatical rules when describing their composition, improvised passage, etc., but these explanations seem to suggest that the musician arrived at the resultant composition or passage by thinking about these rules; often, especially for the very best musicians, musical output is rarely arrived at through the conscious use of complex rule-based systems—like speaking in one's native language, the best musicians do what "sounds right," operating based on native-language-like intuition rather than complex rule-based systems.

I am not suggesting that you should avoid any rule-based system for understanding or performing music, but such rules should always be accompanied by an aural understanding of the forms from which these rules are derived. The more developed your ear is, the less need you will have for a complex list of prescriptive rules or systems. Following the method in this book, you will likely be able to create the musical structures that would arise from these rules without consciously following any rules, the same way you adhere to grammatical rules in your native language without needing any conscious knowledge of how these grammatical rules operate.

CONSCIOUS THOUGHT

Practicing the exercises in this book will require significant conscious thought and intentional mental effort, which is necessary to reconfigure your mind to process music optimally. While reconfiguring your mind will require considerable mental effort, you will ultimately use very little conscious thought when engaging in actual musical tasks, with such tasks eventually feeling quite effortless. Conscious thought and strenuous effort will be necessary to perform these exercises because they will force you into a new way of thinking about musical sound and notation. Most musicians have unknowingly built inefficient cognitive systems for processing music, and these inefficient systems might feel secure because of their familiarity; however, this feeling of security is not the same as efficiency. When constructing a new and more efficient cognitive system for understanding music through the exercises in this book, you will lose the apparent security of your prior cognitive system, and this may feel very uncomfortable. Building your new cognitive system will feel challenging, but *using* your new cognitive system will ultimately feel easy.

FUNDAMENTAL SKILL #1: KEYBOARD VISUALIZATION

IT IS necessary to have a framework to understand musical objects and their relationships. A mental representation of a piano keyboard is the most practical framework for this purpose, and the ability to maintain a mental representation of the keyboard is the first fundamental skill necessary to achieve musical fluency. A robust visual representation of a piano keyboard in your mind gives you an internal instrument that can be mentally "played." The piano keyboard is an ideal instrument to visualize because of its extensive range and capacity for polyphony (the ability to play multiple notes simultaneously). The keyboard is also clearly laid out regarding relationships between high and low notes: higher notes to the right and lower notes to the left.

You do not have to be a pianist to build a mental model of the piano keyboard. Pianists may have a head start in building this model, but many pianists have a surprisingly weak mental representation of the keyboard. Try to have your visualized keyboard active whenever you are interacting with music, whether you are sight-singing or playing an instrument, improvising or reading music, composing, listening, etc. You should imagine "playing" the mental representation of the keyboard whenever you engage with music, even if you are not a pianist. At first, visualizing the keyboard while playing a different instrument may seem challenging, but it will eventually become second nature. The visualized keyboard should also be as vivid as possible when performing a sight-singing or dictation task. Think of your mental keyboard as the cognitive device that will process music before it reaches your actual physical instrument, whatever that instrument may be.

At advanced stages of keyboard visualization, your visualization may be fluid—you may "zoom in" or "zoom out," and it may change shape, size, color, viewing angle, etc. The process of building a mental model of the keyboard may be alternatively thought of as "keyboard spatialization," allowing for a clear conception of where all the notes are and the relationships between them, even if that conception feels less literally visual. It is unlikely that blind pianists have a literal visual representation of the keyboard; more likely, their representation is spatial. That said, imagining a visual representation of a piano keyboard is generally the most straightforward way for most people to acquire a spatial understanding of the keyboard.

The best musicians often visualize their instruments without even realizing they are doing so. When asked if they visualize their instrument (or if they *could* easily visualize their instrument if prompted to), most great musicians will answer affirmatively—some would become quite incredulous if you were to tell them that there are musicians who *cannot* visualize their instrument. Most great musicians did not intentionally develop this ability, but because most great musicians started training very young, they conceptualized the music-learning process in this visual/spatial way in which many children are prone to learn. Children who instinctively visualize their instrument achieve success and are considered talented, while children who do not visualize their instrument struggle mightily—they often feel untalented and eventually quit playing music. I want to emphasize that this difference is not innate—it arises from how a child just happens to start thinking about music. Anyone of any age can develop the ability to visualize the keyboard, just like the young learners who unintentionally engage in this practice.

Mental Practice

Through practice, you will eventually be able to "play" your mental keyboard fluently and easily; it should be easier than playing an actual keyboard instrument, considering there are no physical/muscular constraints on the mental keyboard. If your conception of what a piano keyboard looks like is initially weak, it is perfectly fine to practice building your mental keyboard near an actual keyboard instrument or image thereof, glancing at it occasionally to confirm your mental representation. Your visualization of the keyboard should soon be so strong that you can "play" your mental keyboard without visually checking a physical keyboard.

If you are a pianist, having a robust mental model of the keyboard will help your piano playing, especially your sight reading. If you are not a pianist, having a robust mental model of the keyboard will enable you to play simple music on keyboard instruments with relative ease, even with little to no physical practice on the instrument. Playing an instrument can be physically challenging, but you must know what notes to play before you can conquer any physical/technical challenges on your instrument. If your brain does not know what notes to play, your hands certainly will not know. You need not imagine your hands on the keyboard while visualizing the keyboard because hands have physical limitations that should not be present in your mind. Keyboard visualization is necessary to track *which* notes you are playing, not *how* you would play them on a keyboard instrument. What your visualization looks like in your mind may vary, but if you consistently try to imagine notes and their placement on the keyboard, your capacity for keyboard visualization will constantly improve. Practicing the keyboard visualization exercises will help you develop your visualization of the keyboard, but do not expect to attain a perfect visualization of the keyboard immediately.

Intervallic Reading and Clefs

You should perform all music reading with the assistance of the visualized keyboard. Whenever you read music, you must visualize it on the keyboard to consider the task a success. A primary reason for this is that music-reading tasks should performed through interval recognition. That is, note identification should mainly be done by recognizing interval distances between notes rather than noticing the absolute position of each note on the staff.

You will use your visualized keyboard to identify what note is being played, rather than figuring out what note is played and subsequently finding that note on your mental keyboard or actual instrument. If you use your visualized keyboard to identify notes via interval distance, by the time you know the note name, you already "see" its relationship to surrounding notes on your visualized keyboard. Alternatively, if you were to identify note names by learning each note's position on the staff, it requires another step to locate that note on the instrument and yet *another* step to understand its relationship with surrounding notes. In contrast, reading by interval through keyboard visualization allows you to see the location of each note on your mental keyboard first, facilitating an understanding of relationships between notes; in other words, because you are finding note names by interval, you already know the intervals between each note by the time you identify the note name.

Let's say you see a G on the second line in treble clef, followed by a C in the third space, as in the following example:

Conventional methods for music reading would require you to memorize what note is in each of those locations on the staff, after which you must find each one on your instrument. If you are trying to imagine what the music sounds like without playing it, you must go back and identify the interval between these two notes and figure out what that interval sounds like. However, if you use your visualized keyboard and read by interval, you can identify the G using a single reference point indicated by the treble clef and then notice that the melody moved up a fourth. You can then imagine moving up a fourth on our mental keyboard, arriving at C, knowing not only what note it is but also where it is located on the keyboard, and the relationship between that C and the prior G. The sound of music depends on interval relationships between notes, so developing the ability to recognize and understand interval relationships is crucial for developing musical understanding and audiation ability. The advantages of intervallic reading over note location memorization will become apparent as you practice keyboard visualization exercises.

An additional benefit of intervallic reading is that it facilitates the ability to read in any clef. If you were trying to memorize the note names of each line and space in seven different clefs, considering there are nine notes in each staff from the bottom line to the top line, it would be necessary to memorize sixty-three different note locations to memorize the notes in all seven clefs, without even including notes above the top line or below the bottom line of the staff! Through intervallic reading, *all clefs can be equally accessible to read.* It is necessary to determine your starting note by referencing the clef symbol, but after that, you can identify any note by intervallic identification from prior notes. It is not harmful to have memorized some note locations in various clefs, but this knowledge should never come at the expense of understanding interval relationships between notes. Note identification by interval does not require brute force memorization of any clef; it only requires a strong mental representation of the keyboard and the ability to rapidly recognize interval size, a process that will be explained in further detail in the Practice section of this book. Appendix A shows the different clefs and where the initial reference points are on each.

ANALOGIES

Developing a robust mental representation of the keyboard may initially sound like an unusual strategy for developing musical skills, but the concept is quite reasonable if you consider other ways you operate in the world. Imagine writing your name—hopefully, this feels easy. Imagine turning a doorknob—this should feel similarly easy. Imagine a more complex task: going into your kitchen and making a peanut butter and jelly sandwich; this should not be difficult to imagine, assuming you have the requisite ingredients. Because these tasks are so easy to visualize, they should be easy to carry out. You could probably even perform all these tasks while blindfolded.

Most people can produce mental representations of these tasks, making them easy to perform in the external world. The capacity to confidently engage in a task relies on the ability to create a mental representation of that task. Take a contrasting example: pick a language you do not speak. Imagine picking up a pen and trying to write a sentence in that language—an impossible task, but not because your capacity to physically write the orthography of that language is a problem for your hand. The problem is that you have no mental conception of the language—words, letters, meanings, etc. You might also try to imagine making yourself a peanut butter and jelly sandwich in the kitchen at Buckingham Palace. Unless you are a regular chef at Buckingham Palace, you likely have no mental representation of the kitchen there. It would be a serious challenge if you were blindfolded and had to make a sandwich in that kitchen. It may be possible with a few hours of "feeling around," finding the refrigerator, smelling the contents of jars to identify ingredients, etc.; this exploration would be effective because it would help you build a mental representation of the kitchen, allowing you to make a sandwich, albeit with much more difficulty than doing so in the kitchen in your own home, of which you likely have a much stronger mental representation.

A lack of a mental representation limits the capacity to engage in actions in the external world. To understand, write, sing, or play music, one must have an accurate mental representation of it. This mental representation must be clear and easy to navigate, hence the utility of keyboard visualization. Clearly and accurately visualizing the keyboard is the most crucial skill to master, as it is the scaffolding upon which you can build a clear conception of musical relationships. Even though you might be playing music on an instrument other than a keyboard, keyboard visualization allows you to have a tangible conception of the sounds of the music, allowing for a fluent performance on your chosen instrument. Focused development of your keyboard visualization ability can produce rapid and significant improvements in musical ability.

Visualization techniques are also used by athletes to improve their performance, and high-level athletes often spend time visualizing tasks they would do in competition. For example, a golfer may visualize their swing, or a skier may visualize themselves navigating an entire skiing course. Navigating a skiing course at high speed requires a strong capacity for visualization, much like navigating music at high speed. While there are significant physical differences between skiing and playing music, visualization encourages a robust mental representation essential for the successful performance of any task requiring a high degree of skill.

An excellent analogy for the visualized keyboard is the mental abacus. In some countries, elementary school students learn mathematics by imagining an abacus. The visualized abacus enables these students to solve arithmetic problems very rapidly. The mental abacus is almost perfectly analogous to the mental keyboard; both are concrete visualized tools that track a complex cognitive process. If you watch a child skilled with the mental abacus doing math, you will see how rapidly, accurately, and effortlessly they do arithmetic. Keyboard visualization can enable your performance and understanding of music to reach equal proficiency.

FUNDAMENTAL SKILL #2: REAL-TIME MUSIC READING

THE SECOND FUNDAMENTAL skill necessary for musical fluency is Real-Time Music Reading. Real-Time Music Reading is the ability to vocalize written music notation while following the notated rhythms. Developing this skill will help you read music notation at the same level of fluency with which you would read your native language, allowing you to rapidly translate written music notation to your visualized keyboard. Any real-time vocalization of music **must** be done with the associated visualization of the keyboard.

Exercises for developing this skill involve speaking note names out loud, in time with the music, ultimately doing so as effortlessly as you would read aloud in your first language. When reading music notation, it is necessary to identify what note needs to be played/sung/imagined. If you cannot identify what note you must play, you will be unable to play that note, imagine the sound of that note, or understand the relationship between that note and other notes. Developing this fundamental skill will facilitate consummate musical literacy and is a necessary precursor to reading music notation and hearing it in your mind.

VOCALIZATION AND UNDERSTANDING

Vocalization is an excellent way to facilitate your understanding of notated music. If any musical feature of a passage, such as note names, intervals, rhythms, etc., is hard to vocalize in real time, that is a clear symptom that your understanding of that musical feature is lacking. Thus, vocalization is the perfect test of your understanding of the musical features of any passage and is an optimal way to improve your understanding of those features. Playing a piece of music on a real instrument makes it possible to acidentally play something correctly. That is, you may not know with 100% certainty which note you are trying to play, but you can reach for a note in that general area on your instrument and happen to get it right. Playing a correct note through sheer luck reflects a gap in musical understanding. It is much more difficult to accidentally vocalize the correct name for a note if you are not sure what note it is. If you can vocalize all prominent features of a piece of music (rhythm, note names, interval relationships, etc.) in real time with absolute certainty, it implies that you have a perfect understanding of those features in the context of that music. Accurate and confident vocalization will almost always lead to better playing outcomes on a physical instrument.

SOLFÈGE SYLLABLES

For vocalizing music notation, I highly recommend using **solfège syllables**. Solfège syllables are simply names for the notes in music; English-speaking countries tend to use letter names to refer to each note, while many non-English-speaking countries use solfège names. The word "solfège" is a French word referring to these syllables or the act of music-reading in general. Following is a chart showing how solfège syllables correspond to the letter names of notes, as well as a table with the phonetic pronunciation of each solfège syllable.

```
Solfège syllables: Do Re Mi Fa Sol La Si Do
Letter names:       C  D  E  F  G   A  B  C
```

Pronunciation:

Do	Re	Mi	Fa	Sol	La	Si
Dough	Ray	Me	Fah	Soul	Lah	See

Solfège syllables are more practical than letter names because solfège syllables are much easier to sing, considering they all end with vowel sounds. Try singing the letter "F;" you will see that this would be unwieldy when rapidly vocalizing music. Furthermore, letter names for notes usually imply the natural version of each note. If you are told that a piece of music is in the key of G major, that will generally suggest that the piece is in the key of G-*natural* major. Letter names are also used for chord symbols, reinforcing this suggestion (i.e., a G major chord is a G-*natural* major chord, not G-sharp, G-flat, etc.). Naming letter names with sharps and flats out loud (e.g., saying "G-sharp") when vocalizing note names is possible but often impractical, as the extra syllable required to say sharp or flat (or extra three syllables for natural, double-sharp, or double-flat) would impact the rhythm of the spoken or sung vocalization.

Other vocalization methods that track relationships between notes will be used in the Practice section of this book, but all of them rely on knowing the most basic information about a note: which note is it? You must know what notes are present to understand any relationships between them. Regardless of the vocalization method, any vocalized notes must always be visualized on a keyboard.

You should understand how each solfège syllable corresponds with each letter name, e.g., **Do=C, Re=D**, etc. Once you become comfortable with solfège syllables, simply learn their corresponding letter names and translate between them if necessary. Many musicians use letter names when describing notes, keys, chords, etc., so you should become comfortable translating solfège names to letter names to facilitate communication between yourself and other musicians.

FIXED-DO VS. MOVEABLE-DO

The vocalization system I advocate, where each solfège syllable refers to a fixed note, is called "**fixed-do**." Fixed-do indicates that each space or line on the musical staff in a particular clef is always represented by a fixed solfège syllable, regardless of what key a piece is in; as the name suggests, **Do** (and every other syllable) is "fixed" within each particular clef (see Appendix A for more information about clefs). For example, if a note is on the second line from the bottom on a treble clef staff, we call that note "**Sol**." Even if that note is sharp, flat, or even double-sharp or double-flat, we still refer to that note as **Sol**. Naming notes this way allows for smooth vocalization, even in music with many accidentals. We could specify a note as "**Sol-sharp**" when describing that note outside of a real-time vocalization, but for rapid real-time vocalization, using the solfège syllables alone without naming accidentals is optimal.

Because you will not be explicitly naming the sharps or flats when vocalizing music in real time, it is necessary to keep track of accidentals; fortunately, this is easy with the help of your visualized keyboard. For example, if you encounter a **Sol-sharp**, you should visualize that note in its actual place on the keyboard while you speak (or sing) "**Sol**." Speaking the solfège name while visualizing the specific note on the keyboard makes it possible to efficiently vocalize and mentally track every note. Even though fixed-do solfège syllables on their own do not convey any context or relationships between notes, your visualized keyboard allows you to *see* the relationships between notes while vocalizing. This book will sometimes use letter names for clarity when describing certain exercises, but you should primarily use fixed-do solfège syllables when vocalizing music in real time.

The **fixed-do** system is not to be confused with the **moveable-do** system, where "**Do**" always represents the tonic (i.e., the first note in the scale); as such, the actual pitch of each solfège syllable in moveable-do changes depending on the key. Movable-do can work for very simple music, but if music changes key, contains chromaticism (notes that are not in the key), or if the key is unclear, moveable-do is much more difficult. Movable-do requires the practitioner to always make a resolute determination of key, often requiring analytic work that makes real-time vocalization impractical. This book will not use the movable-do system, but it will use analogous systems for understanding and vocalizing notes' functions within a key. Fixed-do is so valuable because any knowledge of a note's function must be preceded by identifying what that note is. Identification of a fixed-do syllable, i.e., the pitch of a note, does not require an understanding of a note's function, but understanding a note's function does require knowledge of that note's pitch. There is nothing magical about the specific syllables used for fixed-do vocalization, and one could create a new system with the same effectiveness using any arbitrary syllable sounds. Still, traditional fixed-do syllables are used in many countries worldwide, so it makes practical sense to use them for note-name vocalization.

Some readers might be familiar with the syllable "**Ti**" instead of "**Si**." **Ti** usually signifies the use of moveable-do rather than fixed-do solfège, so **Si** will be used throughout this book to remain consistent its standard usage in the fixed-do system.

FUNDAMENTAL SKILL #3: AURAL IDENTIFICATION

THE THIRD FUNDAMENTAL skill necessary for musical fluency is Aural Identification, the ability to recognize, identify, label, sing, and imagine through audiation any musical interval, both harmonic (notes played simultaneously) and melodic (notes played sequentially). This skill is essential on its own, but the Keyboard Visualization and Real-Time Music Reading skills are necessary to apply the Aural Identification skill to the translation of music notation into sound or vice versa.

Understanding the sounds of intervals is essential to produce a proficient musical performance. Many performers barely hear the music they are playing; these performers are just "going through the motions" and engaging in strictly mechanical performances. Some performers do not know what a piece will sound like until they play it —this is better than the former situation, but still not ideal. A performer should know exactly what a piece of music sounds like merely by looking at the notation. A musician should also be able to identify notes in a musical passage upon hearing it. For improvised performances, a musician should know what an improvised passage will sound like before (or simultaneous to) its actual performance. Similarly, a composer should be able to write music without the need to check what it sounds like at an instrument after notating it. The exercises in the Aural Identification section will help develop these abilities.

This third fundamental skill can be the most frustrating to acquire and develop. You must be patient and keep working on it. The most important part of this stage is opening yourself up to new ways of hearing; this will be discussed further in the Practice section, but do not be afraid to listen as a child would. The exercises for this skill will help you achieve a progressively deeper understanding of the sounds of intervals.

ALL IDENTIFICATION IS INTERVALLIC

Any aural note identification, labeling, or sight-singing task is one of interval identification, with the caveat that those with absolute pitch may be able to identify notes without using interval identification. Unless you have absolute pitch, any note identification and labeling task is only possible through interval identification. This may sound like a reductionist view, but if the conception of what qualifies as an interval is sufficiently widened, identification of notes *must* happen via interval— there is simply no other way to do it. Each identification task may use a different reference point, but all note identification tasks are (and must be) intervallic.

Many musicians identify notes by listening for where each note is positioned within a key/scale, a process often called **scale-degree identification** (see Appendix B). The note's position in the scale is aurally identified and then translated into the actual note name. For example, if a musician is listening to a piece of music and hears a note that sounds like the third note in the scale, and the musician knows the piece of music is in the key of C major, they will know that the note they heard was E, the third note in the C major scale. This note was identified through familiarity with the sound of the third note in *any* key; this is incontrovertibly an interval identification task. Listeners identify notes in this way by knowing the sound of each interval above an imagined (or aurally present) tonic (the first note in the scale). Note identification is inevitably intervallic even if the musician does not consciously know any names or labels for these intervals, so a musician might recognize the sound of the third note in the scale without realizing the note's relationship to tonic is giving rise to that identifiable sound. A musical passage must have had sufficient context to establish the sound of tonic to recognize the sound of the third note in the scale; that is, to recognize the aural relationship between the third note of the scale and the tonic, one must also recognize the sound of the tonic.

Perhaps rather than hearing the relationship to the tonic, the musician knew that this note was E because the musician figured out that the prior melodic note was F, the fourth scale degree, and identified the E by noticing it was a half-step below F. Identifying the E in this way is also done by interval identification, albeit with a different reference point. Alternatively, the musician may have identified an A minor chord in the music and heard the E in question in relation to its interval above the chord root A; this is still interval identification but with a completely different reference point. But how did the musician identify the root of the A minor chord? Possibly by hearing the interval of the root A against the tonic C, identifying A as the sixth scale degree. How might a musician realize this chord was minor? By hearing the interval relationships between chord tones, whether they were consciously able to label each one or not. All these identification methods are intervallic but with different reference points through which the interval is identified (see below).

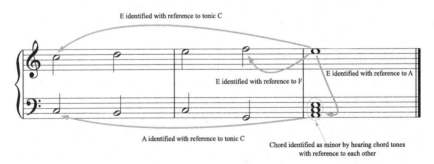

Some popular ear-training methods suggest that you memorize a particular interval by relating it to a piece of music you know very well in which that interval is prominent in the melody. The problem with this strategy is that an interval can sound dissimilar depending on its place in a key or its harmonic context. An interval that might be immediately recognizable in the melody of a famous movie's soundtrack can sound very different in another piece of music (or even in the same piece of music) in a different musical context. Additionally, imagining a different piece of music for every interval you encounter can be excruciatingly slow. I strongly recommend against identifying intervals by relating them to well-known songs.

VERTICAL VS. HORIZONTAL INTERVALS

I refer to intervals as either vertical or horizontal, depending on the reference point used for identification. A vertical interval is based on the relationship between two simultaneously occurring notes. For instance, if you identify a melody note based on its relationship to a simultaneous bass note, that relationship is a vertical interval. Importantly, the reference note does not have to literally co-occur with the target note. When identifying a note based on that note's relationship to the tonic (the first note in the scale), the tonic may not be sounding at that moment; however, the sensation of tonic can be so powerful that a listener can hear vertical interval relationships against an implied or remembered tonic, regardless of its actual audible presence at any moment.

Horizontal intervals are identified based on melodic motion between consecutive notes. In horizontal interval identification, the reference point changes every note—every note becomes the next note's point of reference. See the diagram below for an illustration of each type of interval; horizontal interval relationships are shown by the solid arrows and vertical interval relationships are shown by the dotted arrows.

Identifying intervals by ear is often easier when listening for vertical intervals compared to horizontal intervals because a note and its reference point are simultaneously aurally available in vertical intervals; that is, it is easier to identify a vertical interval because you hear (or imagine, as in the case of the tonic) both notes of the interval simultaneously. Music will also often contain longer-lasting vertical reference points, e.g., a tonic, chord roots, bass notes, etc., granting the listener more constant and stable reference points with which to identify intervals. Below is an illustration of the same melody, with dotted arrows showing vertical interval relationships of each note as related to the tonic:

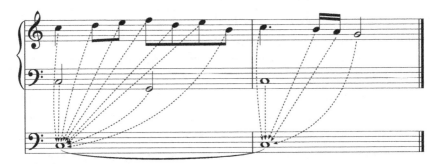

Horizontal identification is generally more challenging than vertical identification because horizontal reference points continually change; each note is a new reference point for each subsequent note. Vertical interval identification against the tonic is usually the easiest way to aurally identify intervals for most music. That said, horizontal identification can be very valuable if the music changes key, contains chromaticism (out-of-key notes), or is not based on conventional major or minor scales. You can identify notes based on either vertical or horizontal intervals depending on what is most practical in any given situation. You will learn to aurally identify intervals both vertically and horizontally in the exercises for Fundamental Skill #3: Aural Identification.

REFERENCE POINTS

You can choose any relevant reference point for interval identification tasks. The tonic is an obvious choice, but chord roots, bass notes, harmony notes, melody notes, or any other perceivable note played by any instrument occurring in the music is fair game when listening for a reference point against which you might identify an interval. Reference points need not occur in direct chronological order. It is possible to hear an interval relationship between notes that occur many measures apart from each other, assuming you have a firm mental image of the pitch of a prior note. It is even possible to use an upcoming note as a reference point; if you are familiar enough with a piece of music and can "hear" a prominent upcoming note in your head, you can identify a note that precedes that upcoming note using the upcoming note as your reference point. You can use any note you are conscious of as a reference point for interval identification.

Combining All Three Skills

It is necessary to develop all three fundamental skills: Keyboard Visualization, Real-Time Music Reading, and Aural Identification. Continually associating your visualized keyboard with vocalized notation and interval sounds will unite them, enabling you to play your mental keyboard just as you would a real instrument.

Think of your mental keyboard as a cognitive tool that will help you recognize note relationships, identify intervals arising from these relationships, and connect each interval to its respective sound. Keyboard Visualization exercises demand explicit note and interval identification, and this knowledge will eventually be fully integrated into your visualized keyboard, making the interval identification process feel automatic. Real-Time Music Reading exercises will help you translate music notation onto your visualized keyboard, connecting notated music with your recognition of notes and intervals. You will begin associating each interval with its corresponding sound through Aural Identification exercises. Once you have developed these skills, you can transfer music notation onto your visualized keyboard, instantly recognizing both vertical and horizontal intervals and knowing their respective sounds, enabling you to hear each note in your mind. This process will initially require intense effort and concentration, but it will eventually feel unconscious and instinctive.

If you are sight-singing a melody, you will be able to play the melody on your visualized keyboard while effortlessly singing each note you are playing. This activity can also be performed silently, allowing you to look at music notation and hear it in your mind without singing it. During a dictation task, the melody you are listening to will appear on your visualized keyboard as you hear it. Of course, this can happen to varying degrees of success—the more rapid and complex the sight-singing or dictation task is, the more difficult it will be to play/visualize on your mental keyboard. Your visualized keyboard should **always** be operative, and your ability to connect your visualization with notation and interval sounds will grow over time, enhancing your musical fluency. I want to reemphasize that this is not a "quick and easy trick" to improve your musicianship. This process can completely restructure how you play, hear, and write music; it may be difficult and frustrating, but it will be well worth the effort.

PART TWO
PRACTICE

PRACTICE OVERVIEW

THE EXERCISES in this book are not meant to be performed strictly in order, except that you must have attained some success with the Keyboard Visualization exercises before moving on to the other two skills. Because the Real-Time Music Reading exercises and many of the Aural Identification exercises demand a constant connection to your visualized keyboard, the exercises for these two skills should only be attempted once you have acquired a rudimentary keyboard visualization ability. This conception need not be robust. After practicing some of the Keyboard Visualization exercises, if you have developed a mental conception of the keyboard, no matter how weak or imprecise, you may move on to the other two skills.

The section for each fundamental skill contains exercises given roughly in order of difficulty. However, you do not need to master any exercise before moving on to subsequent exercises. Most of these exercises are designed so that you may challenge yourself to perform them progressively faster, with increasing complexity, and with more fluency. For easy reference when practicing, a complete list of exercises with a brief description of each is provided in Appendix E at the end of the book.

Your progress with these exercises will likely not be linear. Your performance in some exercises will improve faster than others. Some exercises will initially seem nearly impossible, while others may seem trivial. The difficulty level of an exercise may depend on your prior experience; for example, an exercise that involves improvisation may initially be easier for you if you are a jazz musician rather than a classical musician. If an exercise is challenging, that's great news; you have found a gap in your musical understanding that you can address with that exercise. In general, if an exercise feels very difficult, that exercise will be more valuable to perform than one that feels very easy. An exercise will still be effective even if you can only perform it at an agonizingly slow speed or with relatively low accuracy. In the unlikely event that an exercise is genuinely impossible, which means you are achieving zero percent accuracy no matter how slowly you perform it, do not bother with practicing it; try focusing on other exercises within the same fundamental skill and return to it later. Do not be afraid to practice these exercises out of order, focus on some exercises more than others, etc., but do not avoid any exercise just because it is difficult.

These exercises may initially feel overwhelming. If the instructions for an exercise seem confusing, reread them slowly and look at the example performances of the exercise if applicable. It may also be helpful to look at the simplified descriptions for each exercise in Appendix E.

Even if you can only understand and reliably practice one exercise, go ahead and practice it; every single exercise in this book is valuable for musical development. Remember that these exercises are meant to directly improve your mind's ability to understand musical sound and notation. Because these exercises target specific gaps in your musical understanding, you will really feel your brain working as you practice them. I cannot overstate how difficult some of the following exercises will feel; they will push you completely out of your comfort zone. This is not just true for novice musicians; these exercises can be very challenging even if you have years of musical experience. The best advice I can give you is this: do not give up. These exercises are unbelievably effective if you can push through them. You *will* get better at these exercises with dedicated practice, and any improvement in these exercises will improve your overall musical ability.

There is no set amount of time you should spend practicing. I only recommend pushing yourself to do as much as you can. You would see appreciable progress in just 10 minutes a day of focused practice. An hour a day would be plenty to produce a huge leap forward in your musical abilities. If you are incredibly determined and can manage more than an hour a day, go for it! Whatever amount you practice, you should always be as focused as possible. These exercises will tire you out, so if you find yourself just "going through the motions," you should stop and take a break.

Fundamental Skill #1: Keyboard Visualization

THE FIRST STEP toward developing your ability to visualize the keyboard is to learn the layout of the black keys on the keyboard. Knowing the layout of the black keys is essential because the note names of the white keys are identifiable by their positions in relation to the black keys. If you have access to a keyboard instrument, look at it. If not, look at the image of the keyboard below. Make a mental note of the pattern of the black keys: they occur in sets of two and three. Once you can access a rough visual conception of this pattern, you can move on to further exercises.

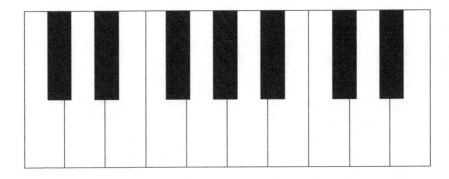

USING THE HAND

When naming notes and "playing" your mental keyboard, it can be helpful to move your hand to follow along with every note you name aloud and visualize on the keyboard. Take your dominant hand and extend your pointer finger, then move your hand left and right following your visualization of the keyboard, but without putting it on an actual keyboard instrument. If you are entirely unfamiliar with the keyboard's layout, you may try this on a physical keyboard, moving up and down the keyboard and resting your pointer finger on each key. If you are a pianist, you may eventually switch to using multiple fingers with more freedom; however, in the early stages, I recommend just using the pointer finger for keyboard visualization, moving left and right with the notes you visualize. Moving your hand will engage your kinesthetic awareness, connecting your sense of movement with the visualization of the keyboard, further reinforcing the visualization. The hand does not need to track every key with precise spatial accuracy, but your hand should generally move in conjunction with your visualization.

THE NATURE OF THE VISUALIZATION

Your visualized keyboard should always be active when engaging in any music task. Consider any exercise you perform ineffective if you are not visualizing the keyboard. From now on, you should connect absolutely everything you do in music to your visualized keyboard. Any time notes are played, imagined, vocalized, written, or heard, you should attempt to visualize them on the keyboard. The visualization may start as a very "zoomed-in" concrete image of one key at a time, and moving around this visualization may initially feel slow. You will eventually be able to manipulate the scale and range of the visualization at your will. Over time, you will be able to "zoom out" and view a progressively larger portion of the keyboard. Do not worry if you cannot do this immediately or even after significant practice—this skill will develop over time. Ultimately, you may even be able to hold multiple simultaneous visualized keyboards in your mind. Do not try to force these more advanced visualizations before you are ready. Visualization ability will come with practice, but you should try to progressively extend the range of what you visualize; if you can only visualize one key at a time, try to be at least aware of the keys directly adjacent. The keyboard visualization exercises will help you construct your mental model of the keyboard and enable you to move around this model. You should not expect to have a clear visualization of the keyboard when you first perform these exercises.

The nature of the visualization may change over time, and the exercises in this section will continuously build and improve your visualization of the keyboard. Your visualized keyboard may eventually feel less concrete and look more amorphous, less like one distinct image of the keyboard and more like an infinitely flexible view where you can rearrange your perspective of the keys at will. Your visualized keyboard may look and feel different as your skills advance, but it is essential to ensure that there is always an active visualized keyboard in your mind, even if it looks or feels different over time.

Solfège Syllables, Preparatory Exercise: Naming Individual Pitches

Once you have some conception of the keyboard's layout, you must be able to identify individual notes. You can do this with solfège syllables, starting with only the white keys. Vocalizing solfège syllables is one of the main activities you will engage in throughout this book. Here is a list of the solfège syllables in ascending order (i.e., moving to the right on a keyboard):

Do Re Mi Fa Sol La Si Do

Begin by speaking the syllables in ascending order from left to right while looking at the above list. Then, try speaking the syllables in descending order, right to left, while looking at the list. You may then visualize them on the keyboard. **Do** is the white key immediately to the left of every set of two black keys on the keyboard. While this note is often referred to as the letter name "C" in the United States, you will usually use solfège names rather than letter names throughout the exercises in this book. The black keys are labeled as "**sharps**" or "**flats**." A black key is either labeled sharp (#) with respect to the white key to the left of it or flat (♭) with respect to the white key to the right of it. Find **Do** on your mental keyboard, follow along with your extended pointer finger, and move to the right one white key at a time, naming every solfège syllable loud until you reach the next **Do**, all the while visualizing the keyboard. Do the same in descending order.

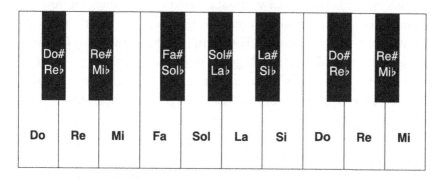

If this is challenging, it may help to imagine the solfège names written on each of the keys on your visualized keyboard. Make sure you notice the position of the black keys in relation to each white key. In the same way that **Do** is to the left of each set of two black keys, **Fa** is to the left of each set of three black keys. Use these two notes as visual reference points to help you find the other notes. You will eventually learn each note's position on the keyboard without needing to move up or down from either of these reference points. Practice each of the keyboard visualization exercises with the aim of maximum fluency, progressively increasing your performance speed when applicable. Remember that you do not need to master any exercise before moving on to others.

INTERVALS

Many of the following exercises will reference intervals. I will refer to the type of interval notation traditionally used in music theory as **conventional intervals** or **conventional interval numbers**. These numbers refer to the distance between two notes. In conventional music theory, intervals have numbers and qualities. For example, musicians might refer to the distance between **C** and **E** as a major third; "major" is the interval quality, and "third" is the interval number. The method in this book will use conventional interval numbers, but it will completely ignore the idea of conventional interval quality.

Conventional interval numbers are named based on how far apart the solfège syllables (or letter names) are, ignoring any accidentals (sharps or flats). These interval numbers are inclusive, meaning you will include both notes in an interval calculation when determining the conventional intervat number. For example, the distance from **Do** up to **Re** is "up a second" and **not** "up one note;" similarly, **Do** up to **Mi** is "up a third," **Do** up to **Fa** is "up a fourth," etc. Below is a diagram showing each type of interval; the bottom note in each set is **Do**:

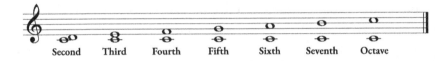

| Second | Third | Fourth | Fifth | Sixth | Seventh | Octave |

The forthcoming exercises will only use six different conventional interval numbers: seconds through sevenths. You will learn to visualize the motion between notes in all these intervals. The interval of an octave consists of two of the same note name; thinking about movement between one note and a higher or lower version of itself is usually straightforward, so exercises will not focus on octave motion.

It is important to remember that conventional interval numbers are always counted inclusively; the starting and destination notes are both included in the number. This can feel counterintuitive at first, but you can think of conventional interval numbers as being determined by counting from one note to another. For example, if you start on **Do** and count up to **Sol**:

```
Do up to Sol:       Do  Re  Mi  Fa  Sol
Interval numbers: 1   2   3   4   5
```

Because this adds up to five, the conventional interval number for the interval that spans from **Do** up to **Sol** is a fifth. Always include the starting note when counting conventional interval numbers. Keep in mind that conventional intervals change when notes are inverted; for example, **Do** down to the **Sol** below it is a fourth, not a fifth:

```
Do down to Sol:    Do  Si  La  Sol
Interval numbers:  1   2   3   4
```

Keyboard Visualization Exercises, Solfège Syllables

Remember to visualize the keyboard as clearly as you can for the following exercises. Your visualization ability will improve with practice.

1.1) Individual Pitch Naming/Visualization

The most straightforward way to develop your ability to recognize note names is to play one note at a time while naming it out loud with its solfège syllable. You may do this on an actual keyboard instrument or on your visualized keyboard; choose a random solfège syllable and speak its name while imagining its placement on the keyboard. You may look at the diagram of the keyboard in the prior section to help you get started.

If you are initially having trouble finding the target note, you may count up or down from another note, but you should strive to know each note's solfège name immediately. You should do this same task with the black keys as well, playing black keys on a keyboard (or imagining doing so) while speaking their solfège syllables using either their sharp or flat name; that is, if you play the black key directly to the right of **Do**, you may call this note either **Do-sharp** or **Re-flat**—either is fine for this exercise. The next exercise will also address learning note names, so work on both exercises simultaneously. Do not expect to master the locations of all notes on the keyboard in a single day. Be patient with this and all other exercises.

1.2) WHITE-KEY INTERVAL CYCLES

The white-key interval cycles exercise will improve your ability to navigate each interval on your visualized keyboard. Choose a starting note and conventional interval number and speak solfège syllables on an ascending or descending interval cycle from your starting note until you reach your starting note again, all while visualizing the keyboard. With the conventional interval terminology used for this exercise, intervals are counted inclusively; that is, a note's distance to an adjacent white key is a second because the distance includes both notes. Here are some examples of ascending and descending seconds cycles from various solfège syllables:

```
Ascending seconds: Do Re Mi Fa Sol La Si Do
Ascending seconds: Sol La Si Do Re Mi Fa Sol
Descending seconds: Fa Mi Re Do Si La Sol Fa
Descending seconds: Re Do Si La Sol Fa Mi Re
```

I recommend becoming very comfortable with ascending and descending cycles of seconds before moving on to larger interval cycles. This does not take long for most people; you can master this quickly if you run through ascending and descending seconds from various solfège syllables a few times a day.

Once seconds are comfortable, try thirds or other intervals. You can think of thirds as every other white key. Below are some examples of different interval cycles from various starting notes:

```
Ascending thirds: Do Mi Sol Si Re Fa La Do
Descending fourths: Re La Mi Si Fa Do Sol Re
Ascending sixths: Fa Re Si Sol Mi Do La Fa
```

Make sure you remember to visualize this on the keyboard. It is possible to speak these cycles very quickly, but your visualization of the keyboard must be able to follow along; otherwise, you will not attain the maximum benefit from this exercise. Try to speak through interval cycles as fast as possible using all seven starting notes and all seven intervals, ascending and descending. Descending cycles tend to be more challenging for most people, but music contains ascending and descending intervals, so neither should be neglected. Remember that in this method, there are only six types of conventional intervals you will need to master: seconds through sevenths. Change your starting note often when practicing interval cycles.

For more advanced interval cycle practice, once you feel confident with all seven ascending and descending cycles, you may construct more challenging versions of the interval cycles exercise by creating ascending or descending sequences of multiple intervals. For example, you might create an "up a third, down a second" cycle. This cycle, starting on **Sol**, would look like this:

Sol Si La Do Si Re Do Mi Re Fa Mi Sol Fa La Sol

Visualizing patterns that change direction can be challenging, so ensure you are fluent with unidirectional single-interval cycles before attempting multiple-interval cycles. Unless otherwise noted, all of these exercises should be performed in your mind, visualizing the keyboard, but without looking at an actual keyboard. If this is too difficult, you may occasionally glance at a keyboard instrument or the image of the piano keyboard at the beginning of the Keyboard Visualization section, but try to get away from this habit as soon as possible.

1.3) DIRECTED WHITE-KEY TRACKING

The directed white-key tracking exercise will help increase the speed at which you can move around your visualized keyboard. This exercise requires a partner who is familiar with the concepts outlined in this book. No need to worry if you do not have a willing partner—the subsequent exercise will develop the same ability and can be performed without a partner.

To perform this exercise, have your partner give you a starting note. Your partner should then speak instructions for where to move on your mental keyboard using ascending and descending intervals of various sizes. For example, your partner may say, "Start on **Do**: Up a second, up a third, down a second, up a fourth." You should follow every instruction your partner gives you on your visualized keyboard, moving by each interval from each successive note. When you arrive at the final note, speak the solfège name of that note; in this case, **La**. If your partner is skilled enough in keyboard visualization, they will know what note you should have arrived upon. If you were incorrect, you and your partner should reverse engineer what went wrong by finding the specific interval that threw you off and focusing on that interval in this and other exercises. Wait until you are comfortable performing this exercise with smaller intervals before you add larger intervals; in other words, perform this exercise only using seconds at first; when this becomes easy, you may use seconds and thirds, etc.

This exercise improves your keyboard visualization ability even if you arrive at the wrong note. Do not wait until your partner finishes their set of instructions before moving around your mental keyboard— you want to visualize and track each instruction as it happens. If your partner is moving too fast for you to stay with the instructions without a significant delay, they should slow down slightly, but you should always try to push the boundaries of the maximum speed at which you can perform this exercise.

This exercise becomes more challenging with a longer list of instructions and faster delivery. This exercise is also more difficult when larger intervals are used. You may push the boundaries of what intervals you are comfortable with, increase the speed with smaller intervals, increase the difficulty by giving a longer set of instructions, or combine all these challenges. For example, try using only seconds but with a very long list of instructions and at a very high speed; or, you may try mostly sixths and sevenths at a slower speed. The advantage of having a partner is that they can fluidly adjust the difficulty on demand. This exercise should be challenging, but not so challenging that you become lost during every set of instructions. Below is an example of a few rounds of this exercise:

Partner: Start on Do; up a second, up a second, down a third, up a second.

You: Re.

Partner: Good! From Re; up a third, down a fourth, down a fourth, up a third.

You: Do?

Partner: Incorrect; the answer was Si. Your response took much longer for that round compared to the prior round. It seems like fourths might be challenging for you; let's do a few rounds that include fourths where I give you the instructions more slowly. From Si: Up a fourth, up a second, up a second, down a fourth…

1.4) RANDOM NUMBER GENERATOR WHITE-KEY TRACKING

The random number generator white-key tracking exercise is like the prior exercise, but you will use a random number generator to mimic a partner giving you instructions. While you cannot fine-tune the difficulty like you can with a partner, it is effectively the same exercise. To perform this exercise, find a random number generator application and generate a list of numbers, with positive numbers representing ascending intervals and negative numbers representing descending intervals. This list should have a range between, at most, -7 and 7. Each number represents an interval number and direction; positive numbers ascend, negative numbers descend. Choose any white-key starting note and follow the instructions as fast as possible, moving around the white keys on your visualized keyboard. Ignore 0, 1, and -1 (or have your number generator exclude 0, 1, and -1). For example, the number set **3, -5, 1, 4, 7** will result in the following instructions: "Up a third, down a fifth, (ignore 1), up a fourth, up a seventh. If you start on **Do**, you will move through these solfège syllables: **Do, Mi, La, Re, Do.**

If you are not yet comfortable with larger intervals, set the number generator to a smaller range, e.g., -4 to 4, resulting in a maximum interval size of a fourth. Try to generate the longest list of numbers you can handle and try to move as quickly as possible through each interval. You may speak each solfège syllable as you go or only speak the final syllable. Remember to visualize the keyboard throughout. You can even repeat the same sequence of intervals again once you arrive at the final solfège syllable. Below are a few example sets with the solfège syllables you would move through for each set:

Solfège:	Fa	Sol	Mi	Fa	La	Si
Intervals:		2	-3	2	3	2

Solfège:	La	Mi	La	Re	Mi	La	Fa
Intervals:		5	4	4	2	-5	-3

Solfège:	Mi	Re	La	Sol	Mi	Sol	Si
Intervals:		7	-4	7	-3	3	3

1.5) Tracking Line Interval Identification

The optimal way to read music is by interval. You should be reading by identifying the interval distance between notes, moving by each interval on your visualized keyboard, and then identifying the note name by observing that note on your visualized keyboard. You might think about this as reading the space *between* each note to identify each successive note. To read this way, you must first be able to visually identify intervals in music notation—this can be practiced using tracking lines, a method I learned from Marianne Ploger. This exercise will begin the process of connecting your visualized keyboard to music notation.

A tracking line is a staff with rhythmless noteheads and no clef. You will use tracking lines to improve your keyboard visualization and interval reading abilities, but before you can identify notes by interval, you should be able to recognize the interval distances themselves. Tracking lines are useful because they can help you perceive the relationships between notes without the extra challenges present in actual notated music. Tracking lines are classified by the largest interval present on the line; a **seconds** line will contain only seconds, a **thirds** line will contain thirds and seconds, etc. See below for example tracking lines:

Seconds

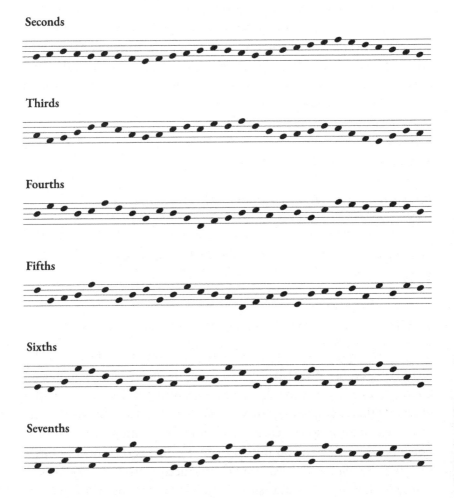

Thirds

Fourths

Fifths

Sixths

Sevenths

You can practice visually identifying intervals by naming the interval and direction of each consecutive note. Start on the first note, identify the interval to the next note, and speak the direction and interval distance; continue this process to the end of the tracking line. See below for examples drawn from the beginning of the sample **seconds** and **fourths** tracking lines:

Seconds

Up a 2nd   Up a 2nd   Down a 2nd   Down a 2nd   Up a 2nd   Down a 2nd   Down a 2nd

Fourths

Up a 4th   Down a 2nd   Down a 3rd   Up a 2nd   Up a 4th   Down a 3rd   Down a 3rd

Because you are not yet naming notes, you do not need to visualize the keyboard for this exercise; just name the interval and direction of each note. This interval identification exercise is one of the few that does not require keyboard visualization.

You may use the sample tracking lines provided or create your own. To create your own **seconds** tracking line, place a stemless note at the beginning of the staff on any line or space; remember, there should be no clef on this staff. Add between twenty-five and forty notes to the staff, with notes moving only by interval distances of a second. The precise number of notes does not matter. Have a good mixture of ascending and descending motion, and try to traverse all the lines/spaces on the staff by the end of the tracking line. You may go one space above or below the staff, but you do not need to move further above or below the staff. The last note on your tracking line should be either on the same line/space as your starting note or an octave above/below. You have now successfully created a **seconds** tracking line! You may do the same for all other intervals. Make sure each tracking line contains a selection of all smaller intervals; for example, a **fourths** tracking line should contain fourths, thirds, and seconds.

If you are having trouble identifying intervals at sight, remember that notes in odd-numbered intervals will be both on a line or both on a space, while notes in even-numbered intervals will move from line to space or space to line; see the following examples:

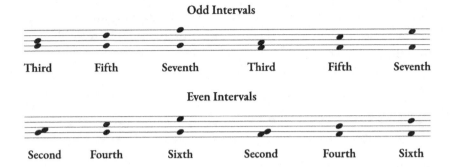

Odd Intervals

| Third | Fifth | Seventh | Third | Fifth | Seventh |

Even Intervals

| Second | Fourth | Sixth | Second | Fourth | Sixth |

If interval identification is difficult, you may start by identifying whether each interval is odd or even, speaking "odd" or "even" for each interval. You do not need to take your visual interval identification ability to an extremely high level before continuing to other exercises—just make sure you can visually identify all intervals (seconds through sevenths) with some reliability, even if it feels very slow. As soon as you can do this, you may continue on to other exercises.

1.6) WHITE-KEY TRACKING, SOLFÈGE SYLLABLES

Once you have gained some facility in visual interval recognition, you may use this recognition to improve your note-identification ability. This exercise will help you visualize and identify the white keys and begin the process of associating musical notation with your visualized keyboard. Start with your **seconds** tracking line and choose any solfège syllable as a starting note. This starting note will be the first note in your tracking line, effectively setting the line to a particular clef (see Appendix A). Avoid choosing a starting syllable that would set the tracking line to a familiar clef; by avoiding familiar note-name placements, you will force yourself to read by interval without relying on prior knowledge of the positions of note names on the staff. You might even find this exercise easier if you are an inexperienced music reader and you are not familiar with any clef! Though you do not necessarily need to know what clef you are using at this stage, a list of relevant clefs can be found in Appendix A.

Once you have chosen a starting note, look at the first note on your tracking line and visualize that note on the keyboard. From there, identify each interval and move around your mental keyboard in accordance with the intervals on the tracking line. Speak the solfège syllable for each note out loud while you visualize each note on the keyboard. Proceed until you arrive at the final note. Remember that these tracking lines only use the white keys for now. See below for an example on the **seconds** line starting on **La**:

Seconds

La Si Do Si La Si La Sol Fa Sol La Si Do Re Do Si La Si Do Re Mi Fa Sol Fa Mi Re Do Si La

The solfège syllables are written in the above example for demonstration purposes, but you should *never* write note names on the staff when performing any exercises. Remember to move your finger/hand in accordance with your mental representation of the keyboard. Every note you speak should be visualized on your mental keyboard, even if the visualization feels weak. The objective of this exercise is not just arriving at the right note—the objective is to improve your sense of interval motion between notes and to associate that motion with your visualized keyboard. Your capacity to visualize will improve over time; it will become easier and the visualization clearer.

You can proceed with the same exercise on other tracking lines or the same line with alternative starting notes. Naming solfège syllables on tracking lines is the main exercise that will promote fluency in associating notes on the staff with visualized movement around your mental keyboard. There is no set way to proceed through white-key tracking exercises, although the larger the interval, the harder each tracking line will be. I suggest not moving on to tracking lines with larger intervals until you can speak every note on an easier line at a comfortable speed, ideally with all seven starting notes. Feel free to move on to a larger interval line even if smaller intervals are slow, but you may find larger interval tracking lines very tedious if you cannot achieve a steady speed on the smaller interval lines. Following is an example of naming solfège syllables on a **fourths** tracking line beginning on **Do**:

Fourths

Do Fa Mi Do Re Sol Mi Do La Re Do La Mi Sol La Do Re Si Mi Do La Re Sol Fa Mi Re Fa Mi Do

You may practice all seven possible starting notes on a particular line; however, if you find yourself memorizing any line, I recommend flipping your tracking lines upside down, as this will give you an unfamiliar order of interval relationships. You may also create a new set of tracking lines if flipping the page upside down feels too familiar. Memorizing a tracking line suggests that you are no longer reading it, defeating the purpose of this exercise.

You can try using a metronome to keep track of the speed at which you can perform these exercises. It is possible to do these exercises at the maximum conceivable speed at which a person could speak solfège syllables—16th notes at 60 beats per minute (i.e., four notes per beat at one beat per second) would be a great long-term objective for the white-key tracking exercises, but it is possible to read tracking lines much faster than that; after all, music routinely contains 16th notes at much higher tempos.

There is no fixed order in which to do the tracking lines. You may find more satisfaction in conquering all seven starting notes on the **seconds** line at a fairly rapid tempo before moving on to the **thirds** line. Alternatively, you may prefer achieving a moderate speed on the **seconds** line using only a few different starting notes before trying to work through lines with increasingly larger intervals. There is no set rule for how to proceed with this exercise. Whatever keeps you motivated and continuing to practice is the best strategy. It is unnecessary to master any tracking line or achieve any specific speed before moving on to the other exercises.

1.7) 15-LINE TRACKING, SOLFÈGE SYLLABLES

The purpose of the 15-line tracking exercise is to force you to read by interval. In a regular tracking line, it can be very tempting to use a prior reference point or calculate the interval from the first note on the line when approaching a larger interval. Many people will avoid direct interval identification to find a subsequent note, instead scanning backward through the line to find a different reference point to use for that note. Scanning backward is not ideal, as it takes the reader back in the notation, disrupting the flow of the music and the visual locus of attention. The 15-line tracking exercise makes this unproductive temptation to look backward nearly impossible. The 15-line tracking staff is simply a tracking line with fifteen staff lines. Because it is so difficult to memorize individual note locations or keep prior note locations in your memory in this tracking line, it forces you to read by interval—there is no other practical way to read a 15-line staff. Treat this exercise just like the regular white-key tracking exercise; try to identify interval distances first, and then choose a starting note and read solfège syllables. Try using a metronome to track your maximum speed with this exercise.

The 15-line tracking exercise will be very difficult if you are not comfortable with the standard 5-line tracking exercise. Constructing 15-line staves on paper or in music notation software can be challenging, but you can get plenty of mileage out of the following 15-line staves, flipping them upside down if you find yourself becoming too familiar with them. Also included are blank 15-line staves for you to create your own 15-line tracking lines.

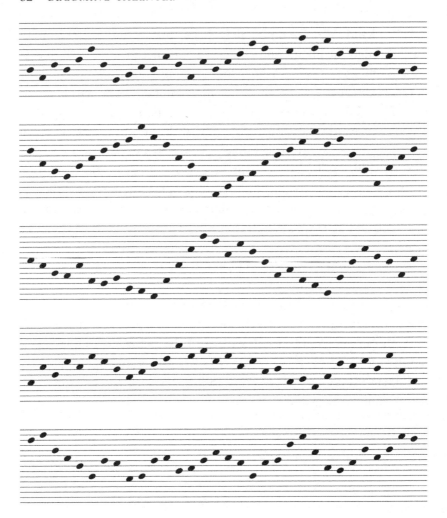

1.8) White-Key 7-Note Row

The white-key 7-note row exercise challenges you to read specific intervals above and below a set of all seven notes, increasing your fluency in rapidly navigating and changing movement direction on your mental keyboard. I learned this exercise from Marianne Ploger, and it is one of the most useful for developing awareness of conventional intervals and their associated motion on your visualized keyboard.

First, randomly write one of each note on a staff with no clef; you should have one of every solfège syllable in any clef you would be in with no solfège syllables duplicated. Make sure there are a variety of intervals between each note you write. This exercise will likely be too easy if you merely write all seven notes as ascending seconds. Choose a starting note and an interval, then speak and visualize the solfège name of that note, move to the note at the selected interval above the written note and speak its name, return to the written note and speak its name again, then move to the note at the selected interval below the written note and speak its name, finally returning to speak the original note's name, all as rapidly as possible while visualizing the keyboard. If possible, visualize the location on the staff of **every spoken note** along with your keyboard visualization. Below is an example of this exercise for the following 7-note row. Do not write solfège names below each note when creating a row; this is for demonstration purposes only.

Do   La   Si   Sol   Re   Fa   Mi

If you select **Do** as the first note, and you choose to perform the exercise using seconds, you would speak solfège syllables as follows:

Seconds: Do Re Do Si Do; La Si La Sol La; Si Do Si La Si; Sol La Sol Fa Sol; Re Mi Re Do Re; Fa Sol Fa Mi Fa; Mi Fa Mi Re Mi.

The same line ascending/descending in fourths would go as follows:

Fourths: Do Fa Do Sol Do; La Re La Mi La; Si Mi Si Fa Si; Sol Do Sol Re Sol; Re Sol Re La Re; Fa Si Fa Do Fa; Mi La Mi Si Mi.

You may also reverse the order and descend first. If you were to use the same row and descend first, vocalization beginning on **Do** would look as follows for seconds and fourths:

Seconds: Do Si Do Re Do; La Sol La Si La; Si La Si Do Si; etc.

Fourths: Do Sol Do Fa Do; La Mi La Re La; Si Fa Si Mi Si; etc.

Keep the direction consistent for the entirety of the row. If you ascend first on the first note, ascend first on every consecutive note; this will ensure you are always aware of which direction you are moving, and you are not accidentally descending when you mean to ascend or vice versa. Try to do this exercise as fast as possible and force yourself to arrive at the notes rapidly, helping to solidify your conception of interval distance above and below each note. Remember to perform this exercise using different starting notes for the same row or create new 7-note rows to avoid memorization.

HALF-STEP INTERVAL (HSI) IDENTIFICATION

AN ESSENTIAL PART of this method is identifying intervals by how many half steps they contain. I will refer to this distance as **half-step interval**, abbreviated as **HSI** or **HSIs** when plural. HSIs will be notated with bracketed numbers. For example, **Do-natural** to **Do-sharp** has an HSI of [1] because **Do-sharp** is one half-step above **Do-natural**. **Do-natural** to **Mi-natural** has an HSI of [4] because **Mi-natural** is four half-steps above **Do-natural**. Unlike conventional interval notation, where interval numbers are inclusive of each note, HSIs are counted exclusively; that is, HSIs label the distance *between* each note. Keep in mind that naming a note with a different solfège name and accidental does not change the HSI of any interval, so **Do-natural** to **Re-sharp** is a [3], as is **Do-natural** to **Mi-flat**; these are equivalent in terms of their HSI but have different conventional interval numbers (second vs. third). There are only eleven HSIs (not including [0], the distance between a note and the same note).

Identifying HSIs improves keyboard visualization. HSI identification is performed by learning what each HSI "looks like" on your mental keyboard. Conceptualizing HSI relationships as visually identifiable entities on the keyboard will force you to visualize the keyboard to complete an HSI identification task. Identifying HSIs is required to know with certainty which intervals you should be singing when performing a sight-singing task. Equally important, each HSI has a distinct sound, and fluent HSI identification is required to recognize HSIs you hear and translate them into specific note names. Do not expect to become skilled at HSI identification overnight. The following exercises will improve your ability to identify and label HSIs, drastically improving your understanding of interval relationships between notes.

The advantage of HSI notation over conventional interval notation (e.g., major second, minor sixth, etc.) as a tool for developing your aural identification ability is that conventional interval notation can refer to the same interval sound using many different labels. For example, using conventional interval terminology, C to F# is called an augmented fourth, whereas C to G ♭ is called a diminished fifth. Using HSI labels, these are both HSI [6] and will thus both sound like HSI [6]. While these two intervals may appear in different contexts, they share the same HSI sound. If you can associate written music notation with your visualized keyboard, you can immediately identify an HSI by "seeing" it in your mind on your mental keyboard, simultaneously associating it with that specific interval sound. Below is a musical passage where vertical and horizontal HSI numbers are labeled. Vertical HSIs are shown with dashed arrows, and horizontal HSIs are shown with solid arrows:

Most music has a clear sense of key; because of this, vertical HSIs related to the tonic (the first note in the scale) can be readily heard and identified. Once the tonic is established, it is possible to perceive vertical HSIs between the tonic and each heard pitch, even if the tonic is not always present; in other words, because the sensation of tonic is so salient, you can hear, identify, and label vertical HSIs between any note and the tonic. The following example is in the key of C (**Do**) major, with dashed arrows indicating each note's vertical HSI relationship to C (**Do**):

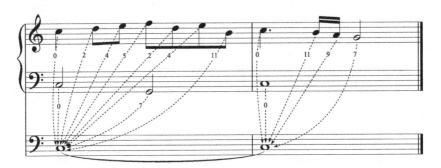

HSI numbers are not octave-specific, so they do not strictly indicate distance per se. **Do** up to **Re** is a [2] whether the **Re** is directly to the right of the **Do** on the keyboard or **Re** is an octave (or more) above. While HSIs are equivalent in different octaves for two notes that are in the same order, an HSI will change if the top note is moved *below* the bottom one or vice versa; for example, **Do** up to **Re** is a [2], but **Re** up to **Do** is a [10].

Each HSI number should be thought of as a category rather than a numerical value. Differences between the sound of each HSI are qualitative and do not gradually change based on numerical distance; that is, proximity does not reflect similarity in sound—a [3] does not necessarily sound more similar to a [2] than to an [8]. This will be discussed more in the Aural Identification section.

1.9) HSI CYCLES

This exercise is like the white-key interval cycles exercise, but rather than choosing a conventional interval number, you will select an HSI number and ascend or descend in cycles. If you choose HSI [2] ascending, starting on **Do**, you will perform this exercise as follows:

```
[2], ascending: Do, Re, Mi, Fa-sharp, Sol-sharp,
La-sharp, Do.
```

If you choose [5] and ascend starting on **Do**, you will get the following results:

```
[5], ascending: Do, Fa, Si-flat, Mi-flat, La-
flat, Re-flat, Sol-flat, Si*, Mi, La, Re,
Sol, Do.
```

The asterisk next to **Si** indicates that the HSI motion remained the same, but the conventional interval number changed, i.e., all the other intervals are named as fourths, but **Sol-flat** to **Si** is a third, not a fourth —this is not a problem for this exercise. This exercise improves your ability to move around the mental keyboard rapidly and understand what each HSI "looks like" starting from any note on your visualized keyboard, so feel free to name whichever solfège syllable is most manageable for mental keyboard navigation. Like the white-key interval cycles exercise, you may also create cycles of multiple different HSIs, for example:

```
Up [3], down [1]: Do, Mi-flat, Re, Fa, Me, Sol,
Fa-sharp, La, Sol-sharp, Si, La-sharp, Do-
sharp, Do.
```

Most HSI cycles will arrive at the original note without cycling through all twelve notes. For example, if you perform an ascending [4] cycle starting on **Do**:

[4], ascending: Do, Mi, Sol-sharp, Do.

You should still be able to speak through these cycles rapidly, making sure you also perform the same cycle starting on different starting notes. Because [4] cycles contains three different notes, there are four different starting notes with which you can begin [4] cycles if you want to cover all twelve notes.

1.10) DIRECTED HSI TRACKING

This exercise is much like the directed white-key tracking exercise where you move around your mental keyboard according to a partner's instruction, but this time, your partner will give you horizontal HSI numbers. For example, your partner might say, "Start on **La**: Up a three, down a two, up a five," to which you would respond with the destination note "**Mi-flat**." If you arrive on a black key, you may speak either the sharp or flat version of that note. Notice the difference in nomenclature in this exercise; "a three" denotes an HSI of [3], while "a third" denotes a conventional interval of a third, which may or may not be a [3]. All recommendations from the directed white-key tracking exercise also apply to this exercise.

1.11) RANDOM NUMBER GENERATOR HSI TRACKING

This exercise is like the random number generator white-key tracking exercise, except here you will generate numbers representing HSIs using a set of numbers between, at most, -11 and 11. You can start with a smaller number generation range to ease into this exercise. You should skip 0 because that represents no motion. Unlike the conventional interval version of this exercise, do not exclude 1 and -1 because these are available HSI numbers. Start from any note, move according to the HSI of each number generated, and speak the solfège name of each note you land on, including sharps and flats. Starting from **La,** the exercise would be performed in the following way if you generated the following five numbers: **3, -5, 8, 1, 2:**

```
La      Do  Sol  Mi-flat  Mi  Fa-sharp
HSIs: [3    -5   8              1   2]
```

You could even move through the same HSI set again when you arrive at the final note. Proceeding through the same cycle from **Fa-sharp** in the above example results in the following extended HSI cycle:

```
Fa-sharp  La  Mi  Do  Do-sharp  Re-sharp
HSIs:      [3   -5  8   1              2]
```

You may use a metronome and gradually increase the tempo to perform this exercise progressively faster. There is no speed at which your performance will be too fast—the faster, the better, assuming you are visualizing the keyboard the entire time. As always, do not speak the name of a note until you can visualize it on the keyboard.

1.12) VERTICAL HSI TRACKING, SPOKEN

In this exercise, you will use tracking lines to increase your awareness of HSI relationships. Start with the **seconds** tracking line to get a feel for this exercise. Choose a starting note and name the vertical HSIs between each note and the starting note. Even if a note is below your starting note on the tracking line, name it as if it were above to mimic HSI identification above an established tonic. In other words, you will be naming the distance from the starting solfège syllable *up* to every single note. Like prior tracking line exercises, you should perform this exercise using only the white keys. See below for an example of vertical HSI tracking on a **seconds** tracking line with the starting note of **Do**:

Seconds, Vertical HSIs

Do 2 4 2 0 2 0 11 9 11 0 2 4 5 4 2 0 2 4 5 7 9 11 9 7 5 4 2 0

Make sure you are comfortable with this exercise on the **seconds** line before moving to tracking lines with larger intervals. Each increase in interval size will result in a significant increase in difficulty. When speaking two-syllable HSIs, shorten them to facilitate rapid vocalization; [7] and [11] can be vocalized as "sev" and "lev." Zero can be vocalized as "oh."

Be aware of all the vertical HSI options with reference to your chosen starting note. For example, if you start on **Do**, your inventory of possible vertical HSI numbers for white keys on any tracking line are [0, 2, 4, 5, 7, 9, 11]. In other words, these are the relationships from the reference point of **Do** to any white key above, so **Do** to **Re** is a [2], **Do** to **Mi** is a [4], **Do** to **Fa** is a [5], etc.

Before you perform this exercise, it can be helpful to speak through the entire ascending and descending white-key vertical HSI inventory from your starting note while visualizing each note on the keyboard. For example, to speak all white-key vertical HSI options from **Do**, speak [0, 2, 4, 5, 7, 9, 11, 0, 11, 9, 7, 5, 4, 2, 0]. The inventory of HSI numbers will change depending on your starting note. For instance, if you select the starting note of **Mi**, the vertical HSI options on the white keys are [0, 1, 3, 5, 7, 8, 10]. Below is an example of vertical HSI tracking on a fourths tracking line starting on **Mi**:

Fourths, Vertical HSIs

Mi 5 3 0 1 7 3 0 8 1 0 8 3 7 8 0 1 10 3 0 8 1 7 5 3 1 5 3 0

1.13) HORIZONTAL HSI TRACKING, SPOKEN

This exercise is like the prior one, but you will choose any starting note and speak the horizontal HSI relationships between each consecutive note. Every number you vocalize will represent the horizontal HSI distance from the previous note. Make sure you are visualizing the keyboard. I recommend only moving on to tracking lines with larger intervals when you become reasonably comfortable performing this exercise at a moderate tempo on smaller intervals. Following are examples of this exercise using a **seconds** tracking line starting on **Do** and a **fourths** line starting on **Mi**:

Seconds, Horizontal HSIs

Do 2 2 2 2 2 2 1 2 2 1 2 2 1 1 2 2 2 2 1 2 2 2 2 2 2 2 1 2 2

Fourths, Horizontal HSIs

Mi 5 2 3 1 6 4 3 4 5 1 4 5 4 1 4 1 3 5 3 4 5 6 2 2 4 2 3

1.14) FULL TRACKING PROTOCOL, SPOKEN

In this exercise, you will vocalize solfège syllables, vertical HSIs, and horizontal HSIs, helping you connect all three vocalization systems. Select a tracking line, choose a starting note, and speak solfège syllables for the tracking line like you would in the white-key tracking exercise. Immediately afterward, perform the vertical HSI tracking exercise on the same tracking line, speaking all the vertical HSI numbers. Next, perform the horizontal HSI tracking exercise on the same line, speaking every horizontal interval. Finally, speak solfège syllables again on the same line. This final step will help reassociate vertical and horizontal HSIs with solfège names on your visualized keyboard. See below for the full protocol on a **seconds** line starting on **Do**:

Step 1: Solfège Syllables

Do Re Mi Re Do Re Do Si La Si Do Re Mi Fa Mi Re Do Re Mi Fa Sol La Si La Sol Fa Mi Re Do

Step 2: Vertical HSIs

Do 2 4 2 0 2 0 11 9 11 0 2 4 5 4 2 0 2 4 5 7 9 11 9 7 5 4 2 0

Step 3: Horizontal HSIs

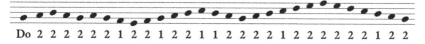

Do 2 2 2 2 2 2 1 2 2 1 2 2 1 1 2 2 2 2 1 2 2 2 2 2 2 2 1 2 2

Step 4: Solfège Syllables

Do Re Mi Re Do Re Do Si La Si Do Re Mi Fa Mi Re Do Re Mi Fa Sol La Si La Sol Fa Mi Re Do

1.15) HSI 7-NOTE ROW

The HSI 7-note row exercise is like the white-key 7-note row exercise, but now you will be naming solfège syllables based on their HSI distance. Create a row with all seven notes written on it and choose an HSI number. Proceed exactly like the white-key 7-note row exercise, naming notes above and below each note, but this time, you will vocalize sharps and flats based on the HSI you selected, making sure you visualize those respective black keys on the keyboard. Try also to name the notes with consistent conventional interval numbers; for whatever HSI you choose, choose a suitable conventional interval number and use that interval to name every note. We can use the same row we used for the white-key 7-note row exercise:

If you select **Do** as the first note and choose to speak solfège syllables for HSI [2] above and below each note, naming each interval in seconds, you will perform this exercise as follows:

```
[2], seconds: Do Re Do Si-flat Do; La Si La Sol
La; Si Do-sharp Si La Si; Sol La Sol Fa Sol; Re
Mi Re Do Re; Fa Sol Fa Mi-flat Fa; Mi Fa-sharp Mi
Re Mi.
```

Consistency of conventional interval numbers is essential. In the above example, you should **not** refer to the **Si-flat** as **La-sharp** because the solfège syllable **La** is a third below **Do**, whereas **Re** is a second above **Do**; this would constitute inconsistent conventional intervals numbers. While **Si-flat** and **La-sharp** look the same on your visualized keyboard, and they are both a [2] below **Do**, you should try to be consistent with both the HSIs and conventional interval numbers for this exercise. It is even possible to do this exercise on [2] while naming your solfège syllables in thirds; though this would be unwieldy, it would look as follows for **Do**:

[2], thirds: Do Mi-double-flat Do La-sharp Do; La Do-flat La Fa-double-sharp La; Si Re-flat Si Sol-double-sharp Si; etc.

These are effectively the same notes as in the prior example, but the solfège syllables are named consistently in thirds; therefore, **La-sharp** is correct here. While awkward, this is something you should be able to do, though it may not be the best use of your time until you reach a very advanced level of keyboard visualization and HSI identification. If consistency with conventional interval sizes (seconds, thirds, etc.) is too difficult, you may start by naming HSIs in this exercise without worrying about consistent interval sizes as long as the HSIs are consistent.

1.16) HSI 21-NOTE ROW

The HSI 21-note row is the definitive exercise for improving HSI fluency; it can be very challenging because it forces mastery of HSIs from every note. I discovered this exercise in Marianne Ploger's book, *The Ploger Method: Crafting a Fluent Musical Mind* (2018), and it is my absolute favorite exercise for developing fluency in HSI idenfitication and keyboard visualization.

This exercise is performed exactly like the HSI 7-note row exercise, but instead of a row containing seven notes with no sharps or flats, you will write out a row that contains one of every single note: sharp, natural, and flat. There should be 21 notes on the staff—seven sharp notes, seven natural notes, and seven flat notes, one of each for all seven note locations on the staff. Select a starting note, an HSI, and a conventional interval number, and name each written note as well as the notes above and below each note in accordance with your chosen HSI and conventional interval number. Ensure you are consistent with the HSI and the conventional interval size. Try to do this exercise as fast as possible. Using a metronome and gradually speeding up the tempo may be helpful. As always, you do not need to master this exercise using all eleven HSIs before moving on to other exercises.

If you choose the starting note **Mi** in the above example (resulting in alto clef) and select an HSI of [3], naming notes in thirds, you will get the following result:

```
[3], thirds: Mi Sol Mi Do-sharp Mi; Si-flat Re-
flat Si-flat Sol Si-flat; Do-sharp Mi Do-sharp
La-Sharp Do-sharp; Sol Si-flat Sol Mi Sol; Si Re
Si Sol-sharp Si; etc.
```

SCALE/CHORD VISUALIZATION

BECAUSE SCALES and chords are the materials used in most Western music, you must be able to visualize them at will. The following exercises will improve your ability to visualize scales and chords. You should be able to easily visualize all major and minor scales (including harmonic and melodic minor). A brief description of major and minor scale construction and a list of all major and minor scales with their accompanying key signatures is provided in Appendix B.

You should also be able to visualize all major and minor triads and all seventh chords. Over time, try to visualize other harmonies such as diminished seventh chords, dominant ninth chords, and even jazz chords (e.g., Maj7#11, etc.); please see Appendix C for a brief overview of chord construction. This book is not designed to explain scale or chord construction in-depth, but the ability to visualize scales and chords can aid in learning music theory and harmony. If you learn more about chords or scales from another source, always visualize any new concepts on your mental keyboard—this will make the learning process much more manageable. As always, if scale/chord construction feels too complicated, skip these exercises and return to them once you have a better grasp of scales and chords.

1.17) Basic Scale Visualization

The best way to begin visualizing scales on the keyboard is to pick any major scale (see Appendix B) and imagine slowly moving through that scale on your mental keyboard, speaking solfège syllables while visualizing the necessary white and black keys for your chosen scale. You may ascend and then descend through each scale on your mental keyboard. You may also improvise, moving at random, up and down, leaping around the scale, etc. Speak the solfège syllables as you move. Imagine the respective white and black keys in your chosen scale lighting up on your visualized keyboard. You may move on to minor scales or any other scale for which you want to increase your fluency.

1.18) Tracking Lines in Key

To further increase your fluency with scales, you may practice tracking lines as previously described, but visualize the accidentals based on the major scale of your starting note. For example, if you select **La** as the first note of a tracking line, you may imagine the **La** major (A major) scale with its three accidentals. You may then perform the full spoken tracking protocol, naming the solfège names, vertical HSIs, and horizontal HSIs, visualizing all three sharps in the key. You may also perform this exercise using minor scales (natural, harmonic, or melodic), making sure you are aware of how vertical and horizontal HSIs differ in each type of minor scale. Below are examples of vertical and horizontal HSIs for a **fourths** tracking line in the key of A (**La**) major.

Fourths, Vertical HSIs

La 5 4 0 2 7 4 0 9 2 0 9 4 7 9 0 2 11 4 0 9 2 7 5 4 2 5 4 0

Fourths, Horizontal HSIs

La 5 1 4 2 5 3 4 3 5 2 3 5 3 2 3 2 3 5 4 3 5 5 2 1 2 3 1 4

SCALE/CHORD VISUALIZATION 79

1.19) CHORD VISUALIZATION

You may follow a similar procedure to improve your chord visualization. Choose a specific chord and speak the solfège names of each note in the chord, with or without speaking the accidentals, visualizing the keyboard as always; see Appendix C for information about chord construction. You should be able to speak a solfège syllable while imagining it on a black key without needing to vocalize its accidental, but you may also speak the accidental name (e.g., "**Fa-sharp**") if it helps you track which note you are visualizing. You must visualize each note in its proper place on your mental keyboard whether you speak the accidental name or not. Once you speak the solfège names, speak the vertical HSI numbers related to the bass followed by horizontal HSI numbers, ascending through each chord tone.

The three-step protocol for chord visualization and vocalization for a B minor seventh chord is below. Letter names are also shown below; letter name notation is often used in jazz or popular music when notating chords, so feel free to speak letter names with accidentals if practical for your primary genre of interest.

Letter Names:	B	D	F#	A
1) Solfège:	Si	Re	Fa	La
2) Vertical HSI:	[0	3	7	10]
3) Horizontal HSI:	[0	3	4	3]

You may also practice this with inverted chords. For example, you can try this on a B minor seventh with D in the bass; some jazz musicians might call this a D6 chord. The protocol will look as follows:

Letter Names:	D	F#	A	B
1) Solfège:	Re	Fa	La	Si
2) Vertical HSI:	[0	4	7	9]
3) Horizontal HSI:	[0	4	3	2]

1.20) KEYBOARD IMPROVISATION

This exercise is performed on a keyboard instrument. A full-size keyboard or piano is ideal, but this exercise could even be performed on a small toy keyboard. Improvising on the keyboard is a great way to improve keyboard visualization because it does not require music reading or aural recognition of intervals. The most important part of this practice is that you must not look down at the keyboard **at all.** I recommend closing your eyes while improvising. Consider blindfolding yourself during this practice if you are too tempted to open your eyes. If you do not have access to a keyboard instrument, do not worry; keyboard exercises are helpful but not strictly necessary to improve keyboard visualization.

To begin practicing improvisation on the keyboard, you can improvise simple melodies with just the right or left hand while visualizing and speaking the name of each note you play using its respective solfège syllable. Because this is happening in real time, you should not speak accidentals (sharps or flats). You may pick a key and try improvising in that key, or you may modulate, use chromatic notes, etc. If you are not comfortable thinking in different keys, just perform this exercise in the key of C major (on the white keys only).

Anything you improvise is fine as long as you are not looking at the keyboard and you are visualizing the keyboard. You may try similar exercises with chords; playing chords with your right hand will be helpful, and you may want to speak the solfège syllables in each chord or speak the name of each chord (C major, E minor, etc.) you play. You should initially restrict chords to a single key (see Appendix C). You may play chords in root position or inversion.

Fundamental Skill #2: Real-Time Music Reading

Real-Time Music Reading is the ability to vocalize a piece of written music in time at the performance speed of the music. This skill will increase music reading fluency and the ability to understand all musical features of notated music in at the performance speed of the music. The "real-time" element of this skill is essential—if you must stop and think about a particular note or passage, it suggests a gap in your understanding of that passage. The ability to fluently vocalize any music guarantees a complete understanding of that music. Vocalization ability does not necessarily immediately translate to an easy performance on an instrument because there may be physical/technical challenges when playing a passage on your instrument; however, knowing what notes to play and understanding their musical context is an essential first step to playing any piece. The physical playing of an instrument is always the last step in the chain of events between music notation and sound, so it is necessary to fully comprehend the written music notation of any passage before engaging in the physical challenges of playing that passage on an instrument.

Your first attempts at vocalizing music in real time might be extremely slow and tedious; this is completely normal. With practice, it is possible to read music very rapidly, as effortlessly as reading your first language. Before describing how to train this skill, I want to emphasize that you can become extremely good at real-time vocalization. You will eventually be able to vocalize complex music at a rapid tempo in any clef. Do not settle for a modest level of development in this skill.

You should develop your real-time vocalization ability even if you primarily engage in a style of music that is mainly improvisatory or rarely transmitted through Western music notation. For example, if you play blues, popular music, improvised jazz, or non-Western music, the ability to read music in real-time is still very useful; understanding music notation gives your mind a concrete way to think about what you are playing, hearing, or composing.

Rhythm Reading

Because all real-time music vocalization must be performed accurately with respect to notated rhythms, your ability to read rhythm notation must be developed to a very high level. You may initially struggle with vocalizing or playing notated rhythms; fortunately, this is one of the most straightforward musical skills to acquire once you have a concrete conception of how rhythmic notation works. Transcribing rhythms you hear can also be quite effortless if you are skilled at reading rhythm notation. Rhythmic fluency/literacy may take some practice, but following the guidelines in this section can enable you to easily perform even the most complex rhythms.

Beats and Subdivisions

Almost all Western music exhibits a sense of beat. Music theorists will happily debate the philosophical or scientific foundations of beats in music, but you can think of the beat as a recurrent pulse that is suggested by elements within the music; more simply, it is the thing you "tap your foot to" when listening to music. The beat is best thought of as the span of time *between* these foot taps; hence, a piece of music is divided into beats that begin at regular intervals of time.

These beats can be subdivided, wherein the span of time a beat is composed of can be further divided into smaller equal chunks of time. Music notation shows how beats are subdivided and where notes occur within these subdivisions. Beats are most often subdivided into either two, three, or four subdivisions; if you master these three types of subdivisions, you will be able to handle at least 99% of the notated rhythms you encounter.

You must first be able to keep a steady beat if you want to understand how to subdivide beats. While sitting, tap either hand on your lap at regular intervals. Most people should not have a problem with this. In the rare case that this is difficult, I recommend listening to a piece of popular music and tapping along to it in this manner. Though many people instinctively tap their feet to music, I generally recommend against using the foot to keep time during rhythm exercises—most people have more precise control over their hands than their feet, so tapping with the hand is generally more practical.

Once you can keep a steady beat, you can practice subdividing each beat. Start by subdividing each beat into two subdivisions. To do this, repeatedly tap your hand on your lap and evenly count to two out loud every time you tap your hand; that is, you will be dividing up the time between each tap into two halves, saying "one" the moment you tap your hand and "two" after you tap your hand. Try not to engage in too much mental work while doing this; most people can complete this task quite easily, and those who find it difficult are often overthinking it— simply tap your hand at a regular rate and evenly count to two each time you tap.

Do the same for subdivisions of three: tap on your lap while evenly counting to three. Next, practice subdividing into four: evenly tap and evenly count to four between each tap. A word of caution: When subdividing into three, be sure that each count is even, i.e., make sure that you are evenly counting to three rather than counting to four with a "silent four."

Once you have completed these steps, perform the same tasks, but this time, instead of speaking numbers, you should speak a neutral vocalization syllable such as "ta." If you can perform all these tasks, you have the basic tools necessary to subdivide beats for almost any music you encounter. Complex classical music, jazz, progressive rock styles, etc., will occasionally subdivide time into other divisions such as five, seven, eleven, etc., but the process is the same for these subdivisions: evenly count the subdivision numbers while tapping the beat.

UNDERSTANDING RHYTHM NOTATION

I will not cover rhythm notation in detail here; instead, I will provide a reliable system for thinking about rhythmic subdivisions. If you have little experience with rhythm notation, feel free to look up the meaning of these symbols in an external source; here, I will focus on how to conceive of rhythm notation in relation to the beat, allowing fluent performances of notated rhythms.

To translate rhythm notation into subdivisions, you must know how written note values divide each beat. The time signature (the two numbers on the staff at the beginning of a piece of music) tells you this information. The top number tells you how many beats are in each measure, and the bottom number indicates what type of note spans the duration of one beat. For example, a 3/4 time signature indicates 3/4 meter, meaning there are three beats in each measure, and a quarter note spans the length of one entire beat. Notes smaller than quarter notes divide the beat into subdivisions, i.e., in 3/4 meter, eighth notes divide each beat into two subdivisions, sixteenth notes divide each beat into four subdivisions, and eighth note triplets divide each beat into three subdivisions.

Therefore, the following passage can be performed by speaking the subdivision numbers out loud while you tap the beat, where "1" always occurs at the commencement of each beat; that is, you will be tapping on every "1":

Try to master switching from each subdivision type to the others. Repeat measure one in the above example a few times and then switch to measure two, maintaining a steady beat. After that, try switching from measure one to measure three. Switching between two and four subdivisions should be easy, but switching to or from three subdivisions will be more challenging. You should practice switching between all three subdivision types. Make sure the beat remains steady and does not slow down or speed up.

Other meters will have different note values representing these subdivisions. In the following example, smaller note values represent two, three, and four subdivisions because each beat spans the duration of an eighth note; that is, in the first measure, dividing each beat into two subdivisions results in sixteenth notes because an eighth note spans the length of one beat in 3/8:

To vocalize more varied and complex rhythms, tap the beat and speak the subdivision numbers that occur in their respective places in the beat while suppressing vocalization of any subdivision numbers that do not coincide with the commencement of a note. It is essential that you still feel each "silent" subdivision number. The grey numbers in the following example represent these silent subdivision numbers—you should speak these numbers "in your head" or feel them just as strongly as the spoken numbers.

In measure one in the above example, the grey eighth rest is still in the "1" subdivision location, but you will not be saying "one" because a note does not occur there. Similarly, in measure two, you should count "1-2-3-4" in your head but only speak the numbers at which notes occur (the black numbers in the above example). You should be tapping the beat on every "1," even if a rest occurs in that space and you are not saying "one." The numbers you are speaking represent note actuation points, i.e., the beginnings of notes. Once you can easily vocalize the actuation points of notes, holding them for their actual value when singing or playing them is not much more difficult.

Before vocalizing or playing any passage, try to work out how each note corresponds with its spoken subdivision number (the black numbers in the prior example); this awareness is necessary for fluent rhythm vocalization. Identifying these numbers is usually straightforward if you understand how each note type divides up a beat. In the prior example in measure two, you can tell that you need to subdivide into four because each beat in that measure contains sixteenth notes, of which there are four in each beat in 2/4. The first eighth note in that measure is a "1" because it occurs on the first of the four subdivisions. If you know that an eighth note takes up the same amount of time as two sixteenth notes, you know that you will not speak the "2" in that subdivision because the eighth note is still sustaining through the "2." The subsequent "3" and "4" encompass the subdivision's third and fourth sixteenth notes, which should both be vocalized.

If a passage is difficult, you may tap smaller subdivisions in the beat instead of tapping only at the start of each beat. For instance, in measure two in the previous example, you may tap four times for each beat (i.e., tapping once on each of the black and grey numbers) to help you keep track of your subdivisions, silently counting numbers where notes do not occur and speaking numbers out loud where notes do occur. Once this is easy, return to tapping at the commencement of each beat. When a passage is easy to vocalize this way using subdivision numbers, you may switch to vocalizing it on a syllable such as "ta."

For smaller note values, you may need to think about dividing subdivisions into further subdivisions. In the above example, you can subdivide each eighth note into four to facilitate reading the thirty-second notes, as if reading this passage in 4/8 rather than 2/4. Tapping each subdivision rather than each beat can be especially helpful in situations with very small rhythm values, but you should always be able to return to tapping the actual beat to maintain the feeling of the written meter. It can take some time before you can instantaneously figure out the subdivision numbers of any passage, but with practice, you should be able to read/vocalize/play most rhythms you come across. You should always continuously tap the beat while vocalizing; alternatively, if you have experience conducting or playing classical music, try to conduct the beat instead of tapping it. The best way to practice vocalizing rhythms is to take real musical examples and vocalize them, first speaking subdivision numbers and then speaking "ta" or any other easily vocalized syllable.

VOCALIZED FEATURE STACKING

VOCALIZED FEATURE STACKING is the primary exercise that will develop your ability to read music in real time. To perform this exercise, you will vocalize music using different vocalization systems, each focusing your attention on a different musical feature. Fluency in real-time vocalization is a clear indicator of musical understanding; vocalizing a feature will direct your attention toward it, ensuring an understanding of that feature. Vocalizing these musical features is considered "stacking" because each feature is successively vocalized, effectively adding a new layer of musical understanding for each feature you vocalize; this will unite your conception of every feature and build a complete understanding of note names and interval relationships. With practice, you will be aware of every feature regardless of which vocalization system you are using. Every feature must be clear in your mind to guarantee a robust understanding of the music.

You should begin by vocalizing monophonic (i.e., one note at a time) melodies. You may find melodies in any music you enjoy, with the caveat that more complex music with rhythmic difficulties, modulation, chromaticism, etc., will be more difficult. I suggest you become reasonably comfortable with melodies that do not change key or have chromatic notes before trying more complex melodies. Exercise complications created for sight-signing practice can be great material for practicing real-time vocalization. Specifically, there are many excellent exercises in the French pedagogical tradition. French music training in the nineteenth and early twentieth centuries focused on vocalizing via fixed-do solfège syllables, so exercises in that tradition are perfect for this task. You can find many compilations of music reading exercises of progressively increasing difficulty if you look for books with "solfège" in the title. I have included references for a few of these compilations in the bibliography.

The syllables in the vocalized feature stacking exercise should be vocalized spoken rather than sung; you should initially refrain from trying to sing so you can focus on accurate spoken identification. To be able to sing anything, you must know what you are trying to sing; thus, speaking is recommended to identify all musical features as a precursor to singing. You will develop the ability to accurately sing pitches in the exercises for Fundamental Skill #3: Aural Identification. You will combine all three skills into sight-singing in the Synthesis section of this book.

To perform vocalized feature stacking, vocalize a passage of music using each of the vocalization systems listed below, speaking each syllable in time with the music. You must visualize the keyboard for all features other than rhythm. Rhythm and solfège syllables should almost always be attempted first and in that order, but you may vocalize other features in any order that helps increase your understanding of the music. It is not always necessary to vocalize every feature, but you should be able to vocalize every feature. It is unnecessary to go through the process of vocalizing a particular feature if you are confident it will be easy, but some features may be much more challenging than you anticipate.

1) Rhythm
2) Solfège Syllables
3) Scale Degrees (if applicable)
4) Vertical HSIs (if applicable)
5) Horizontal HSIs

Extra:
6) Jazz/Pop Chords
7) Miscellaneous Features

The first five features are most important; the extra features, six and seven, might be practical depending on what sort of music you are vocalizing and what your goals are regarding the performance of your selected passage, but they will likely not be necessary for the bulk of your vocalization practice. Rhythm and solfège syllables must be vocalized in time and at tempo, but you do not necessarily need to vocalize every other feature up to tempo; vocalizing a feature at a slower tempo can still crystallize your knowledge of that feature.

2.1) RHYTHM

The most crucial feature for vocalization is rhythm. To vocalize rhythm, speak a sound in real-time for every note that occurs. The syllable "ta" works well, but any syllable is fine. You may even use different syllables, e.g., "ba, da, ta," if you are trying to make your rhythm performance more musical or emphasize specific notes. Tap or conduct the beat while vocalizing to ensure you are vocalizing rhythms accurately and fluidly. The beat should not slow down or stop during vocalization; if it does, your rhythmic understanding of that passage needs clarification. Many passages may look rhythmically simple but might be surprisingly tricky to vocalize. Sometimes, vocalizing a single measure with rhythmic accuracy might be easy, but fluently vocalizing that measure in its surrounding context may be difficult. Try to vocalize the entirety of a musical passage without any pauses or hesitation.

If you have little music-reading experience and reading rhythms is extremely difficult or confusing, you may approximate rhythms as best you can and focus on other features, returning to focus on accurate rhythm vocalization once you have a better grasp of rhythm reading. If you have trouble vocalizing a passage using "ta," start by vocalizing subdivision numbers as described earlier. Once subdivision numbers are easy, switch back to "ta."

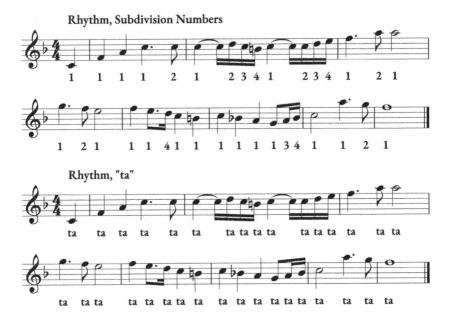

2.2) SOLFÈGE SYLLABLES

To vocalize solfège syllables, speak each solfège syllable in accordance with the notated rhythms. There should be no dissipation of your visualized keyboard at any point. All further vocalized features rely on the fluent vocalization of solfège syllables because accurate solfège vocalization necessitates identification of the pitch of every note. Even the slightest hesitation when vocalizing solfège syllables suggests a problem with note identification. If you have trouble vocalizing solfège syllables, try moving on to other features, vocalizing them slowly, and then return to speaking solfège syllables. Other vocalization features may help you visualize the keyboard more clearly, improving solfège recognition. If vocalizing any syllable in time with the beat is difficult, you may temporarily attempt to vocalize syllables without regard to rhythmic accuracy, but you should try to vocalize with the correct rhythms and a steady beat as soon as possible. Following is the prior example melody with solfège syllables notated under the staff:

2.3) SCALE DEGREES

Speaking scale degrees will be helpful for music that has a clear sense of key. Scale degrees are numbers associated with the position of each note in a key; see Appendix B for more information about scale degrees. If a passage contains a chromatic alteration, you may vocalize the altered scale degree without verbally indicating the accidental, but make sure you visualize the actual note on the keyboard. For example, in the key of G Major, the notes C C# D can be vocalized "4, 4, 5," despite C# being a raised fourth scale degree. Speaking "four" for both C and C# is not a problem if you visualize C# on your mental keyboard while vocalizing "4." If a passage changes key, reassign scale-degree numbers to notes in the new key. If you are unsure exactly where the key change occurs, switch to solfège syllables until you establish a sense of key again, then switch back to scale-degree numbers.

It is not always necessary to vocalize scale degrees, and it is not practical or useful for many pieces of music, especially if the music does not strictly conform to major or minor keys. It is most beneficial to vocalize scale degrees if an unmistakable sense of key is present in the music— you do not need to try to force scale degrees onto music that does not have a clear sense of key. The example melody is in F major; each note should be vocalized with its numerical position in the key. Scale-degree four appears in its altered and unaltered forms; you may vocalize "four" for both, but make sure you visualize the actual position of the note on your mental keyboard when vocalizing.

Scale Degrees

2.4) VERTICAL HSIs

For vertical HSI vocalization, base your HSI selection on whatever vertical relationship is useful. The most straightforward way to vocalize vertical HSIs is to use the tonic as the reference point. If the melody you are reading has a written accompaniment featuring a bassline, chords, or other potential vertical relationships, you may also speak vertical HSIs as related to any other relevant reference points. The following melody in the key of G major can be vocalized with vertical HSIs [0, 4, 5, 6, 7] as related to the tonic G:

You may also base your vertical HSI judgments on any other prominent vertical relationship in the music. In the same example, notice how the A bass note is held under the C and C#—this may be vocalized using vertical HSIs [0, 4, **3**, **4**, 7], naming the C as [3] and C# as [4] with respect to the A bass note, and then returning to tonic as a reference point when you arrive at the D (see below):

The D could also be vocalized as [0] with the bass note D as a reference point, which would be especially useful if you want to consider this passage as modulating to the key of D. If the passage changes key, you may change your HSI reference point to that new key. This process is discussed further in the Synthesis section.

Whatever HSI reference point you choose, visualize the spoken note without losing track of your reference point, visualizing both notes on the keyboard if possible. Make sure you shorten "zero," "seven," and "eleven" to "oh," "sev," and "lev" to avoid difficulties vocalizing accurate rhythms. Some music may not contain salient vertical relationships. If this is the case, vocalizing vertical HSIs may be more trouble than it is worth; however, all but the most atonal music will contain some relevant vertical relationships through which vertical HSI vocalization may be helpful for a portion of the music. See below for the example melody notated with vertical HSIs with reference to the tonic:

2.5) HORIZONTAL HSIS

Vocalizing horizontal HSIs is like vocalizing vertical HSIs but will be done with less freedom in selecting reference points; for horizontal HSIs, every note becomes the subsequent note's reference point. To vocalize horizontal HSIs, you will name HSIs between each consecutive note. Remember that HSIs only go up to [11] and do not increase further with additional octaves, e.g., **Do** up to **Do** an octave above is HSI [0].

All melodies can be vocalized with horizontal HSIs. Doing so is invaluable because it will improve your keyboard visualization and interval identification abilities; both are necessary for sight-singing and audiation. Vocalizing horizontal HSIs may feel overwhelming at first; continued practice of horizontal HSI vocalization of melodies as well as the HSI exercises for keyboard visualization will improve your fluency. See below for the same melody labeled with horizontal HSIs:

2.6) JAZZ/POP CHORDS

If you work with jazz, popular music, or any other style that uses chord charts, you can vocalize the chords in real time like other features. One strategy is to speak each chord name in time with the music when each chord occurs. To further increase understanding, you may choose a single chord tone and speak solfège syllables or letter names of that chord tone. For example, you may choose to speak the letter names or solfège syllables (with or without accidentals) of **the third** of each of the following chords:

Chords:	Dmaj7	Emin9	A9	Dmaj7
Chord 3rd:	F#	G	C#	F#
Solfège:	Fa-sharp	Sol	Do-sharp	Fa-sharp

Vocalizing every chord tone (root, third, fifth, seventh, and beyond) can help solidify your knowledge of each chord. Visualizing the entire chord on the keyboard can be helpful even when vocalizing only one specific chord tone. Speaking any of the above syllable options is useful, but it can be practical to use letter names instead of solfège syllables because chord symbols are usually notated using letter names. You may also rapidly vocalize and visualize all notes in each chord in ascending or descending order, although it may be impractical to vocalize this in real time if the chords are changing very rapidly. For jazz musicians, vocalizing a walking bassline or other quasi-improvised chord-related features may be helpful. See Appendix C for more information about chords.

2.7) MISCELLANEOUS FEATURES

Vocalizing any other applicable features in the music may be done at your discretion. For example, you may wish to vocalize harmonic elements such as chord Roman numerals. If you are working on a technically demanding passage on your instrument, you could vocalize fingering numbers or another technical feature that applies to your instrument. You even want to vocalize dynamic choices ("piano... forte..."). Whatever you vocalize, make sure it is done in real time while tapping or conducting the beat—do not stop or hesitate at any point. If you do, slow down and work on the passage until you eliminate all hesitation. Try to vocalize any significant or challenging features in any music you want to play or understand. As always, visualize the keyboard.

VOCALIZATION CHALLENGES

It is not necessary to vocalize every single feature for every passage of music, especially if vocalizing one of the suggested features looks trivial; however, you might be surprised by a feature that halts the rhythm of vocalization or makes visualization of the keyboard difficult. For example, you might find that speaking horizontal HSIs on a particular melody looks easy, but when you try it, you lose track of the visualized keyboard. You should consider all vocalization tasks (except for rhythm-only vocalization) unsuccessful if you lose your keyboard visualization.

If vocalizing any feature presents a problem, you can isolate the difficult portion of the passage, slow it down, and vocalize somewhat out of time. Gradually return to rhythmic accuracy once you have a firmer grasp of the feature you are vocalizing. You must read and visualize every passage; do not just memorize it and repeat a vocalization syllable sequence by rote. If any feature is significantly more challenging to vocalize than solfège syllables, that often indicates a gap in your understanding of that feature, and you would benefit from practicing it. Do not overestimate your ability to vocalize any feature.

POLYPHONIC MUSIC READING

VOCALIZING music at tempo is impractical for polyphonic music (i.e., music with multiple simultaneous notes) because it is only possible to vocalize one syllable at a time. Fortunately, there are ways to improve your polyphonic music reading regardless of how many simultaneous notes are present. To practice polyphonic music reading, you can vocalize one part while imagining that part and all other parts of the music on your mental keyboard. This task can be very challenging if you are not reasonably skilled at vocalizing monophonic melodies. Spend a lot of time vocalizing monophonic melodies before adding polyphonic music to your vocalization practice. The following exercises will hone your ability to read and understand polyphonic music.

2.8) POLYPHONIC SOLFÈGE/HSI VOCALIZATION

One of the best exercises to ensure maximum fluency in polyphonic music is vocalizing solfège syllables and vertical HSIs in polyphonic music. To perform this task, you must rapidly name the solfège syllables of every note. You cannot do this in real time because multiple notes sound simultaneously; despite this limitation, rapid vocalization is valuable to promote instantaneous note identification. You can vocalize solfège syllables from the lowest note to the highest. In the example below, each chord can be vocalized bottom to top, starting with the lowest note in each chord:

Sol	La	Si	La
Re	Re	Re	Re
Si	La	Sol	Fa
Sol	Fa	Sol	Re

```
Bottom to top:
Chord 1: Sol Si Re Sol
Chord 2: Fa La Re La
Chord 3: Sol Sol Re Si
Chord 4: Re Fa Ra La
```

It is also valuable practice to vocalize the outer voices first, naming the notes in the lowest voice, then the highest voice, and then all notes in between, descending from high to low, while adding each note you vocalize to your visualized keyboard. For example, in a piece of music with typical four-part harmony, you could name notes in the following order: bass, soprano, alto, and tenor (bottom, top, second from the top, third from the top). In the above four-part example, you can vocalize one chord at a time with the outer voices first as follows:

```
Outer voices first:
Chord 1: Sol Sol Re Si
Chord 2: Fa La Re La
Chord 3: Sol Si Re Sol
Chord 4: Re La Re Fa
```

When vocalizing music in which voices are rhythmically offset, you should name any notes present as a vertical sonority, even if they are held over from a previous moment. See the following example. You may vocalize each sonority from bottom to top or with outer voices first. As always, the solfège syllables written below the staff are for demonstration purposes only; never write solfège syllables, HSIs, etc., on a score.

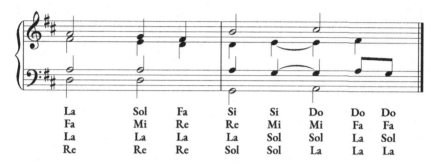

La	Sol	Fa	Si	Si	Do	Do	Do
Fa	Mi	Re	Re	Mi	Mi	Fa	Fa
La	La	La	La	Sol	Sol	La	Sol
Re	Re	Re	Sol	Sol	La	La	La

Bottom to top:

Re La Fa La; Re La Mi Sol; Re La Re Fa; Sol La Re Si; Sol Sol Mi Si; La Sol Mi Do; La La Fa Do; La Sol Fa Do.

Outer voices first:

Re La Fa La; Re Sol Mi La; Re Fa Re La; Sol Si Re La; Sol Si Mi Sol; La Do Mi Sol; La Do Fa La; La Do Fa Sol.

Vocalizing outer voices first is valuable because those voices are usually the most prominent and aurally salient musical features in most pieces of music. The outer voices can also help you frame your visualization; the identification and visualization of the outer voices can help you visualize the inner voices in relation to the outer voices. You can practice this exercise by proceeding through music one vertical structure at a time. Perform this task as rapidly as possible, and you could even practice with a metronome, gradually increasing the tempo.

You can practice this same way with keyboard music containing multiple simultaneous melodies. For example, if you are naming solfège syllables in the first measure of Bach's Invention No. 1 in C major:

Do Re Mi Fa Re Mi Do Sol Sol Do Do Si Si Do Do
                        Do Re Mi Fa Re Mi Do

This would be read as follows, with the bottom notes first, including all vertical sonorities:

Do Re Mi Fa Re Mi Do **Sol** Do **Sol** Re **Do** Mi **Do** Fa **Si** Re **Si** Mi **Do** Do **Do**

You should vocalize any notes that are actuated *or* held; in other words, you should vocalize any note that would be aurally present, ensuring that you keep visualizing each note for its entire duration. The bold notes in the above example are the eighth notes in the right-hand part. These notes are repeated because they are held during the moving sixteenth notes in the left hand.

Naming solfège syllables is a helpful first step for this practice, but naming all vertical HSIs as related to bass notes can be more challenging and will further solidify your keyboard visualization; because HSIs are identified through your keyboard visualization, naming vertical HSIs ensures that you are visualizing every single note. You may name HSIs from bottom to top or with the outer voices first.

Feel free to name any other vertical HSIs if you have trouble identifying or visualizing a particular note; for example, you can name vertical HSIs between an inner voice and the top voice if you are having trouble keeping track of the movement of those voices. Naming HSIs against the bass is generally the most useful practice because of the importance of the bass in most music. Rapidly naming all vertical HSIs on the score ensures a complete and fluent understanding of the vertical intervallic relationships in the music. Following is the prior four-part example shown with vertical HSIs above each bass note:

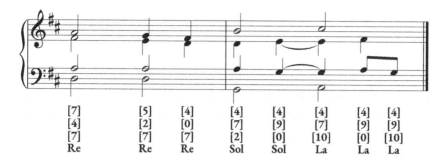

Bottom to top, vertical HSIs:
Re 7 4 7; Re 7 2 5; Re 7 0 4; Sol 2 7 4; Sol 0 9
4; La 10 7 4; La 0 9 4; La 10 9 4.

Outer voices first, vertical HSIs:
Re 7 4 7; Re 5 2 7; Re 4 0 7; Sol 4 7 2, Sol 4 9
0; La 4 7 10, La 4 9 0; La 4 9 10.

This can be practiced similarly for polyphonic piano music. The first seven notes in Bach's Invention No. 1 do not occur with any simultaneous notes. You can just name these notes as solfège syllables or even horizontal HSIs, switching to vertical HSIs when the bass notes appear:

In two-part music like the above Bach Invention, there is no difference between vocalizing bottom to top or outer voices first. This excerpt would be read as follows using solfège syllables and vertical HSIs, vocalizing all vertical sonorities. The bold HSI numbers represent each vertical HSI between simultaneous left-hand and right-hand notes.

Do Re Mi Fa Re Mi Do Sol Do [7] Re [10] Mi [8] Fa
[6] Re [9] Mi [8] Do [0]

Polyphonic vocalization exercises can be challenging, but these exercises are essential because naming vertical HSIs of every vertical structure encourages a clear visualization of the entirety of the music without losing track of any notes.

2.9) ADVANCED KEYBOARD IMPROVISATION

You should attempt increasingly more advanced keyboard improvisation practice once you are comfortable vocalizing polyphonic music. Try playing chords with your left hand while you improvise a melody in your right hand. The chords may be played as block chords or as a rhythmic accompaniment pattern if your hands are up for the task. This should all be attempted with your eyes closed. Below is an example of three different left-hand patterns for playing chord progressions:

The most effective and challenging way to use a keyboard instrument to stretch your visualization ability is by playing a stride pattern in your left hand while improvising a melody in your right hand. In a stride pattern, the left hand plays the bass note of a chord followed by the full chord higher up on the piano. You should attempt this with your eyes closed. Playing a stride pattern with your eyes closed will be very challenging at first, but it will force you to visualize large portions of the keyboard. You can do this at an extremely slow tempo if necessary. If it is too challenging to play a stride pattern while improvising a melody, try working on the left-hand stride pattern without impro-vising a right-hand melody. See below for a sample left-hand stride pattern:

Playing a stride pattern with your eyes closed may feel excruciatingly slow at first. Take your time and slowly "feel around" for every single note if necessary. When locating a particular note, feel for the sets of two and three black keys to orient yourself; find the intended notes using those kinesthetic reference points. This exercise aims to build a more robust mental visualization of the keyboard, not to play virtuosic stride piano. If you look at the keyboard while playing, you are no longer building a mental model of the keyboard—you are simply navigating a model you are looking at. Playing a stride pattern on the piano with closed eyes can be extremely difficult, even for experienced pianists. Do not expect this ability to be quickly or easily acquired, but simply attempting this exercise with your eyes closed will improve your keyboard visualization ability regardless of your level of success at playing the stride pattern. Attempt these improvisation exercises in every key.

2.10) KEYBOARD SIGHT READING

The ability to sight-read music at the keyboard is incredibly useful even if you are not a pianist. Practicing the exercises in the Keyboard Visual-ization and Real-Time Music Reading sections will improve your ability to sight-read at the keyboard, even if you have never touched a keyboard instrument. Playing music at sight on the keyboard is a beneficial prac-tice because it will allow you to produce polyphonic music (i.e., music with multiple notes at once) on a real instrument if your primary instru-ment is monophonic (i.e., only able to play one note at a time). Hence, a rudimentary ability to sight-read on a keyboard instrument is valuable even if piano is not your primary instrument. Make sure you are comfortable with real-time vocalization before attempting to sight-read on the keyboard.

To sight-read on the keyboard, it is important to develop your ability to not look down at your hands. Obviously, this ability cannot be helped by closing your eyes or blindfolding yourself as in prior improvisation exercises because sight reading requires you to look at the music you are reading. There is a solution to this problem: place a bed sheet, blanket, apron, etc., over your hands and the keyboard while playing, a strategy purportedly used by renowned music teacher Nadia Boulanger to help her students improve their sight reading. Make sure whatever object you use is not so heavy that it interferes with your hands while playing. It can help to tuck one side of the sheet into your collar or wrap it around your shoulders so it is lifted off the piano and does not interfere with your hands.

You should become comfortable reading and playing monophonic melodies in one hand before attempting music for two hands. While sight reading, you may speak the solfège syllables of any notes you are playing while you play them. Whatever you do, do not look at the keyboard, even if you must laboriously feel around the piano keys to find each note. You will achieve a better mental conception of the keyboard every time you feel around for the correct notes. If sight-reading on the keyboard is entirely too frustrating, practice more keyboard visualization and eyes-closed improvisation exercises. Remember that playing piano is not required to follow the method in this book, so do not worry if you do not have access to a keyboard instrument; you can still make excellent progress without practicing any keyboard sight reading.

Maintaining continuity is essential when sight reading. Avoid pausing, hesitating, or "double checking" any notes you play. Try to count the beat (or subdivisions thereof) out loud without ever stopping or slowing down the beat, and try to ignore any wrong notes you play; this will force you to continue without hesitation. Even if your note recognition ability cannot keep up with your counting, try to visually follow along in the score in accordance with your count, playing whatever notes you can and leaving out any notes you cannot identify rapidly enough. Even if you must leave out all the notes for many measures at a time, try to fluidly continue through the score while counting, coming back in whenever you can. Avoid moving backward, restarting, or repeating any notes.

You can also practice real-time vocalization of polyphonic music in conjunction with keyboard sight reading. While you cannot simultaneously vocalize multiple syllables, playing one part of the music while vocalizing another is entirely possible. To do this, play one part while you speak (or sing) solfège syllables of another part, in time with the music while visualizing the keyboard; for example, you might play the left-hand part of a piece of music while vocalizing the solfège syllables of the notes in the right-hand part. If the music you are trying to play is very challenging, you may simplify it for this exercise by selectively leaving out notes; however, you should still strive to play in time and keep a steady beat. Playing bass notes while vocalizing the melody and removing inner voices is often the most straightforward way to simplify polyphonic music on the keyboard, especially if you have minimal keyboard skills. You may also do this exercise while vocalizing HSIs, either horizontal or vertical, from any relevant reference point.

You can practice sight-reading any music in this way. Bach's four-part chorales are great practice, playing one voice (or more) while speaking (or more advanced, singing) another. You can use any combination of voices for this practice, but I suggest playing the bass while vocalizing the top voice (and vice versa) before trying other combinations. For more advanced practice, you can play popular or classical songs for voice and piano this way, playing the entire accompaniment while vocalizing the melody using solfège syllables. Compositions for piano and a single monophonic instrument (e.g., flute sonatas, violin sonatas, etc.) are also suitable for practicing keyboard playing with vocalization. These challenges require very advanced development of the three fundamental skills, so do not feel discouraged if you cannot accomplish any of these tasks even after considerable practice.

It is possible to play and vocalize full orchestral scores, string quartets, etc., facilitating a deep understanding of all parts of complex pieces of music. I recommend becoming extremely skilled at vocalizing single-note melodies before you attempt to read/play multi-instrument scores. You may use any combination of vocalization methods that are helpful while vocalizing and playing challenging multi-instrument music. It is possible to play an entire reduction of an orchestral score while speaking (or even singing) the solfège syllables for a single part, all upon first looking at the score (i.e., with no prior preparation). This can be very challenging, but you can develop the ability to perform these tasks if you practice the exercises in this book. Playing full orchestral scores on the keyboard while singing one unplayed part should be considered the highest challenge to test your development of the three fundamental skills. You should not attempt to sing your vocalizations for any of these tasks before spending a considerable amount of time practicing the exercises for Fundamental Skill #3: Aural Identification.

Fundamental Skill #3: Aural Identification

Aural identification is the skill that will allow you to aurally identify intervals, enabling you to identify notes upon hearing their relationships to other notes. This skill will also help you accurately sing or imagine the sound of any note in any musical context. The exercises for the prior two fundamental skills help you identify notes and intervals on your visualized keyboard and associate them with music notation, and exercises for this third fundamental skill will help you understand what these notes and intervals sound like, combining your visualized keyboard with an awareness of music notation and musical sounds. Developing this skill through brute force and repetitive practice is more challenging than it is for the prior two fundamental skills. This skill requires you to pay attention to what intervals *feel* like. I use the term "feel" because many who struggle with this skill, especially adult learners, try to "listen harder" to interval sounds they hear to identify them. Rather than thinking about the *sound* of any interval, think about the *feel*. The word "feel" is not used here as a metaphor for emotion but rather as a metaphor for physical sensation; that is, to feel in the tactile sense of the word. While this may sound nebulous, it is an excellent way to start exploring your awareness of interval sounds. Listen for the quality of an interval, *not* how far apart notes are from one another. In other words, try to identify a single visceral sensation that results from the interaction between two notes.

Developing this skill is all about training your perception. These exercises will initially feel very uncomfortable, and some may even seem impossible. All intervals may sound the same to you at first. You will improve if you continue to do the exercises. You can ultimately learn to differentiate, label, hear, and sing all eleven intervals, even if you can barely differentiate two different intervals at first. The exercises in this section consist of either aural interval identification or interval singing, but you need not practice these exercises in any specific order. If an exercise feels completely impossible, return to it later after working on other exercises. The first two exercises for this fundamental skill are better accomplished with a partner. You can still make excellent progress without these two exercises, and you can simulate these two exercises with computer software, so there is no need to worry if you do not have a willing partner for practice.

To help you understand what it is like to hear and identify different intervals, consider the analogous task of identifying and labeling colors. When most of us see colors, we can easily name them. Looking more closely at a color or spending more time thinking about which color you are looking at does not contribute to accurate color identification. Many of us would be at pains to even describe how we know which color is which. Try to describe what purple looks like without referencing other colors—you will notice what a challenge this is. When identifying colors, we "just know" what they are, principally because they were pointed out to us as young children. Most of us have not had the analogous experience of having musical interval sounds pointed out to us at a young age, but an understanding of the qualitative elements of musical intervals can be introduced and mastered at any age. A very young child is rarely frustrated if they cannot immediately accurately label every color they see upon first learning the concept of color; similarly, you should not be frustrated upon realizing you cannot immediately aurally identify and label every musical interval you hear. Identifying and labeling interval sounds may have never occurred to you before; you may have never thought to listen to musical sounds this way, and this practice may be entirely new. It may take a while for you to achieve any success with these exercises, but please be patient with yourself. Remember that the ability to differentiate and label intervals does not rely on innate talent; anyone is able to acquire this skill.

Many of these exercises require singing. Do not worry about the sound of your voice for these exercises—just attempt to sing the correct pitches. If you have minimal singing experience and have trouble matching pitches, try playing a note on a keyboard while you sing a note, sliding the note you are singing up or down until the note you are singing matches the note you are playing. With practice, you will be able to match pitches quite easily. Do not worry if this remains difficult. Developing your ability to differentiate interval sounds will improve your ability to match pitch. There is no need to sing a note in its proper octave for any of these exercises, so feel free to sing any note in any comfortable octave. For example, if an exercise calls for a **Sol** too high for you to sing, you may sing any lower **Sol**. For any of the following exercises that involve singing, you may check your sung notes by playing them on the keyboard after you sing them; however, try to do this as infrequently as possible, even if you feel very uncertain about the notes you are singing.

Some of these exercises require an understanding of scale and chord construction. Appendix B contains rudimentary information about scale construction, and Appendix C describes chord construction. Do not worry if you do not understand this material; skip the exercises that require this knowledge and return to them once your knowledge of scales and chords advances. It is possible to have an extremely well-developed ear with very little knowledge of music theory.

3.1) VERTICAL IDENTIFICATION OVER A DRONE

This first exercise will introduce you to the aural identification of vertical HSIs over a stable reference point, which will help you aurally identify notes as related to a tonic. In this exercise, the reference point will remain stable and audible as a continuous drone note, making it easier to hear, identify, and compare vertical HSIs. This exercise is best performed with a partner, but you may perform this exercise on your own if you can produce a drone note and use a software application to generate notes.

To begin, hold down a low **Do** (C) on a keyboard, ideally an octave or two below the **Do** (C) in the middle of the keyboard. The instrument producing the sound does not matter; you may sustain this note on a piano (replaying the note when it dies out), play it on another instrument, or digitally generate it with a synthesizer using a sustained sound such as an organ, string section, etc. Have your partner (or a note-generating application) play any notes in C major (i.e., the white keys) over the drone while you attempt to identify scale degrees out loud (of course, without looking at what notes your partner is playing on the keyboard). Your partner can play one note at a time or multiple successive notes for a greater challenge.

You should also perform this exercise by naming notes according to their vertical HSI numbers. You do not have to master this exercise using scale degrees before trying it using vertical HSIs. Switch between scale degrees and vertical HSIs for successive practice sessions. Before vocalizing HSIs, it can be helpful to run through the possible vertical HSIs in the major scale: [0, 2, 4, 5, 7, 9, 11].

Try to visualize the keyboard for any note you hear or label, even if you are not sure if your label is correct. If you have a partner, tell them to slowly move through notes in the same octave without jumping around too much, i.e., use mostly seconds motion up and down the scale rather than larger interval leaps. If this is too difficult at first, narrow down your selection of notes to only two or three different notes. **Do, Re**, and **Mi** (scale-degrees one, two, and three) would be good choices at first. If you identify a note incorrectly, your partner should play your guess and the target note back-to-back, comparing them, after which you can make another attempt. Singing each note you hear can be very helpful for this exercise. Once you have some accuracy in labeling scale degrees and HSIs, you may switch to solfège syllables.

This exercise may initially seem difficult, but you should achieve a reasonable level of accuracy in a short amount of time. If you feel confident naming solfège syllables in C major, you can switch the drone and key to another major key (see Appendix B), identifying and naming solfège syllables, scale degrees, or vertical HSIs in that new key. Make sure you can visualize the new key on the keyboard. The only vocalization syllables that should change when changing keys are your solfège syllables; every major key has the same scale-degree numbers (one through seven) and vertical HSIs [0, 2, 4, 5, 7, 9, 11].

Once you feel confident in major keys, switch to minor keys over a drone, keeping in mind that the vertical HSI inventory will change—make sure you are acutely aware of what your new HSI inventory will be and try to visualize each scale on the keyboard. You may practice this exercise using natural, harmonic, or melodic minor, or a combination of all three. Continue to name vertical HSIs normally, but when naming scale degrees in minor keys, you can say "sharp six" for the raised sixth scale degree in melodic minor, etc. You may also name full solfège names (e.g., **Sol-sharp**) to specify chromatic alterations like those occurring in minor keys. The specific naming convention you use is less important than your ability to identify the note accurately and visualize it on the keyboard. If using diverse major or minor keys feels too complicated, do not worry; this exercise is still beneficial even if you only attempt it on the white keys in the key of C major.

When you have become comfortable with major and minor keys, you may add chromatic notes (i.e., notes outside of the seven notes in the scale) to both major and minor keys, still holding a single drone note as a reference point. You should incorporate one chromatic note at a time rather than adding all of them to your inventory of possible notes. For chromatic notes, naming vertical HSIs will be the most useful because vertical HSIs ignore issues of enharmonic spelling (i.e., sharps vs. flats), but naming solfège syllables with or without accidental names is also suitable. Performing this exercise using all eleven HSIs may be difficult; as always, it is not necessary (or even recommended) to master this exercise before moving on to other exercises for this fundamental skill.

3.2) PLOGER INTERVAL DRILLS, HARMONIC INTERVALS

In this exercise, you will have a partner play isolated intervals for you to identify by ear using HSI numbers; this will train your ability to aurally identify intervals using constantly changing reference points. I have titled this exercise "Ploger Interval Drills" because it is based on exercises employed by music pedagogue Marianne Ploger. If you are having trouble with the aural interval identification exercises in this section, I recommend her book, *The Ploger Method: Crafting a Fluent Musical Mind* (2018), in which she describes specific perceptual features of interval sounds and provides strategies that may help you differentiate them.

For this exercise, your partner (or a software application) will play two simultaneous notes, referred to as a "harmonic interval," and you will speak the HSI number of the interval you think you heard. If you are correct in your identification, your partner should move on to another set of notes. If you are incorrect, your partner should play the interval you named related to the lower note of the original interval as an opportunity to correct you. If you are generating intervals using a digital application, this correction stage is not possible; however, this exercise can still be effective without the real-time correction of a partner.

A sample round might proceed as follows: Your partner (or digital interval generator) might play A and C at the same time. Immediately speak the HSI you think you just heard. If you hear this as a [3], say "Three" out loud, and your partner should play two other simultaneous notes, which may be the same or a different interval for you to identify. If you thought you heard a [4] and said "four," your partner should immediately play A and C#, showing you your mistake. Ideally, you might realize that is a [4]. In this case, you should say "four," and your partner should return to the original interval, which hopefully you now realize is a [3], which you should state out loud: "Three!" This process should move rapidly, shooting for speeds of one interval per second or faster. Most intervals played should have a different bottom note, resulting in a new reference point every time. Do not think about what interval you are hearing—respond as fast as you can, even if it feels like you are guessing. Do not try to "listen harder" to any interval sound you hear, as this will make the identification process more difficult. As soon as an interval sound hits your ear, everything you need to identify that interval is already available to your mind.

You should start by comparing only two intervals. For example, you might pick [1] and [7]. Your partner should proceed to play a random selection of [1] and [7] intervals:

{E, F}, {F, C}, {A#, B}, {B, C}, {G#, D#,}, etc.

The notes in each set should be played simultaneously, and you should respond immediately after each interval played, naming the HSI you think you heard. Your partner may present a comparison for you at first, e.g., "This is a [1] (plays {B, C}), this is a [7] (plays {B, F#}), etc." Below is a list of recommended interval sets in order of difficulty. Start by comparing set one until you feel confident, then move on to set two, and so on. This progression may take many weeks or perhaps even months (or longer) before you are able to perform this drill with all eleven intervals with any accuracy. Feel free to alter these sets or their order at your convenience; I am presenting them only as a starting point, as this list starts with intervals that most listeners would find easier to discriminate at first, increasing in difficulty for each subsequent set. If you often confuse a specific interval for another, isolate those two intervals and spend time comparing only those two intervals.

1) [1] [7]
2) [1] [4]
3) [1] [10]
4) [1] [11]
5) [6] [7]
6) [2] [7]
7) [2] [3]
8) [2] [4]
9) [2] [11]
10) [2] [10]
11) [10] [11]
12) [1] [2]

```
13) [1] [2] [10] [11]
14) [1] [2] [6] [7]
15) [1] [2] [6] [7] [10] [11]
16) [5] [6] [7]
17) [3] [4]
18) [1] [2] [3] [4] [5] [6] [7] [10] [11]
19) [8] [9]
20) [3] [8]
21) [4] [9]
22) [4] [8]
22) [3] [4] [8] [9]
23) All 11 HSIs
```

For those who find this exercise incredibly challenging or if all intervals sound the same to you, I recommend drilling only intervals [1] and [7], without moving on to other intervals until you can accurately discriminate between [1] and [7] at least 90% of the time. For most people, [1] and [7] are the easiest intervals to tell apart; developing the ability to identify just these two intervals should help you understand what it feels like to aurally identify intervals. Equally important, it will give you the confidence to continue developing your interval discrimination abilities. Do not worry even if you cannot discriminate [1] and [7] at first; everyone can learn to hear, identify, and label these eleven interval sounds.

You may feel discouraged if you find this exercise very challenging. Reframe your struggle as an opportunity to hear and understand elements of music that you have yet to perceive. Many experienced musicians cannot even differentiate [1] and [2], which is surprising considering major scales are entirely composed of horizontal HSIs [1] and [2]. Most musicians have played major scales hundreds if not thousands of times, but many have never opened their aural perception to hear the horizontal interval content of major scales.

You should not expect to become skilled at this overnight. Remember that this is the ultimate challenge for your ear. Constantly changing intervals with constantly changing reference points is about as hard as it gets for aural identification, and most "real life" aural skills tasks do not require such perceptual virtuosity. This exercise aims to help you explore perceptual differences between intervals—the objective is not just to "always get the right answer." Even the slightest improvement in performance in this exercise means you have unlocked a new capacity of your aural perception. Even a *decrease* in accuracy can imply improvement because this often suggests a fundamental change in the way you are listening to interval sounds; this is almost always followed by an ensuing increase in accuracy. A temporary dip in accuracy is especially likely if you had prior aural skills training taught inefficiently or insufficiently. You may need some time to undo previous inefficient methods of identifying and labeling interval sounds.

You should experiment with compound intervals (i.e., intervals with notes separated by more than an octave) in this exercise. Remember that interval sounds are equivalent in multiple octaves if the notes are in the same order, e.g., C up to any higher E is [4], but C down to any lower E is [8]. If the order of notes changes, the interval will change (except for [6], which inverts into a [6], e.g., B-F and F-B are both [6]). Compound intervals can emphasize certain qualities of each interval sound, making some easier to identify. I especially recommend listening to compound versions of [1], [3], [5], and [8]. Qualitative features of these intervals often sound more obvious in compound form than when the notes are in the same octave.

You are not trying to identify the "distance between" two notes; instead, you are trying to identify characteristic qualities of each interval sound. When performing this exercise, try to respond as quickly as possible. Avoid thinking about the identification task as much as you can. You will soon discover that excessive conscious thought during this exercise will tend to interfere with your ability to differentiate and identify intervals.

3.3) INTERVAL DRILLS, MELODIC INTERVALS

You may eventually move on to melodic intervals, i.e., one note played after another, naming HSIs like in the prior exercise. I only recommend trying this once you achieve a high level of accuracy in harmonic intervals; specifically, do not attempt to identify melodic intervals for any set of intervals before you can identify harmonic intervals of that same set with at least 80% accuracy. For example, if you can differentiate and correctly label [1] and [7] as harmonic intervals with at least 80% accuracy, you may attempt to compare ascending or descending melodic versions of [1] and [7]. Pick only one direction at a time at first; for example, if you are comparing [1] and [7] as melodic intervals, compare only ascending [1] with ascending [7] at first—do not compare ascending intervals to descending intervals in the same round of the drill until you are very comfortable differentiating intervals in only one direction at a time. You must become comfortable with harmonic intervals before melodic intervals because interval identification relies on identifying characteristic traits of each interval; these traits can be heard most clearly in harmonic intervals. You can recognize these traits in melodic intervals by keeping the first note of each interval in your memory for each melodic interval, essentially simulating a harmonic interval.

Melodic intervals can be more challenging to identify, so you should ease into melodic interval identification by holding the first note of each interval while playing the second. Doing this lets you hear the melodic interval while hearing the harmonic interval you should already be comfortable with, slowly moving you from harmonic to melodic identification. For example, if playing a melodic ascending [7] on C and G, your partner should play C followed by the G above while continuing to hold down C, which presents both a melodic and harmonic interval sound. This will help you start to relate the sound of the melodic interval to the harmonic interval you can already identify.

3.4) Interval Drills, Three or More Notes

You can also perform harmonic interval drills with more than two notes at once. Have your partner play three or more notes and identify the vertical HSIs related to the lowest note. For example, if your partner plays C, F, and G#, you should respond with [0, 5, 8]. Accurate HSI identification can be challenging with multiple notes because multiple levels of interval relationships occur; a [3] also occurs between F and G#. If you hear C, F, and G#, and your answer is [0, 5, 3], do not think of this as a failure; instead, you correctly identified the HSIs between each note instead of the HSIs with reference to the lowest note. All of these interval relationships are musically relevant within this set of three notes. You may even try to name only the interval between a particular subset of the notes, e.g., only between the highest and lowest notes.

Your partner may play these notes with any spacing. It might be easier to play the lowest note relatively low on the keyboard and any other notes separated by an octave or more; feel free to be creative with variations on this exercise. If you correctly identify the HSIs, your partner may tell you the bottom note name ("C"), whereby you can identify the other two notes by visualizing the HSIs above the bottom note: [5, 8] above C: "F, G-sharp!" Feel free to use solfège names or letter names during this task. I recommend attaining high accuracy in identifying all eleven HSIs for two-note harmonic drills before moving on to three or more notes. You may also experiment with melodic interval sets of three or more notes, though this may be very difficult without considerable mastery of harmonic interval identification.

3.5) VERTICAL IMPROVISATION OVER A DRONE

Improvisation is one of the best ways to improve your ability to sing and imagine interval sounds. Start by holding a drone note on a keyboard instrument, initially in a key with few sharps or flats (see Appendix B) to make keyboard visualization easier. Sing any vertical HSI number above your drone, all while visualizing the keyboard, proceeding to another note if you feel confident. You might start by only singing notes from the major scale, vertical HSIs [0, 2, 4, 5, 7, 9, 11]. Make sure you are always singing the HSI number that occurs *above* your drone, i.e., if your drone is C, singing E should always be thought of/heard as a [4] (interval above C) rather than [8] (interval below C), regardless of the octave in which you are singing. You may also sing using scale-degree numbers.

Pay attention to the way each sung note feels against the drone and try to hear the sound that results from the interaction between the drone and your sung note. If you are trying to sing a particular vertical HSI but are unsure of the target pitch, just take a guess and check your sung note on the keyboard afterward. Make sure you give yourself enough time to securely sing the target note before checking it on the keyboard. If you check a note and realize you did not sing the intended pitch, correct yourself and match the note on the keyboard. Give your ear some time to absorb these sounds. As always, the purpose is not just singing the right note—deepening your aural perceptions is the central aim of this exercise.

If you are comfortable singing vertical HSI numbers and scale-degree numbers, you may switch to singing solfège syllables to facilitate more rapid improvisation, but make sure you are visualizing the specific note you are singing on the keyboard. If you are singing solfège names, you should still be aware of the vertical HSI numbers; you must have some awareness of the HSI number of the note you are singing to accurately sing the solfège syllable because that HSI number represents your conception of the relationship between the drone note and your sung note.

If improvisation in major keys is comfortable, try the same exercise in minor keys, using natural, harmonic, and melodic minor, still holding a tonic drone. You may also try the same exercise using an HSI inventory that will result in modal improvisation. For example, you might sing only white keys over a drone on the note D. This would result in the dorian mode rather than a major or minor scale. If performing modal improvisation, it can be helpful to name all the possible vertical HSI numbers you might sing. If improvising on the white-key notes over a D drone, you would have an HSI inventory of [0, 2, 3, 5, 7, 9, 10]. Always be aware of the HSI inventory of any scale or mode you are using. Feel free to incorporate all eleven vertical HSIs once you confident improvising vertical HSIs in key.

3.6) HORIZONTAL IMPROVISATION

If you are comfortable singing vertical HSIs with the support of a drone, you may try improvising using horizontal HSIs. Play any note on the keyboard and sing any horizontal HSI number above or below this note while visualizing the sung note on the keyboard. You may sing multiple notes in succession in this exercise. Try to limit your HSI options when you first attempt this exercise; for example, you might improvise using only ascending and descending HSIs [1] and [2]. Every time you sing a note, play it on the keyboard to check your accuracy and hear it as your new reference point against which you will sing your next horizontal HSI. In other words, "chase" your sung notes on the keyboard after you sing them. If you sing a wrong pitch, simply match the note played on your keyboard to correct your error and continue with your improvisation. You will make many mistakes when first attempting this exercise, but do not worry; you will improve with practice. Feel free to switch to singing solfège syllables if you are always aware of their respective horizontal HSI numbers. The melodies you create while improvising horizontal HSIs can contain chords and parts of scales, or they can be completely atonal, leaping through any horizontal HSIs at random. Take note of any HSIs that you repeatedly sing incorrectly and perform this exercise emphasizing those intervals. Also keep track of specific challenges in HSI direction. For example, ascending [7] might be easy, but descending [7] might be more difficult.

For a greater challenge, play your starting note and improvise sung horizontal HSIs between each successive note *without* chasing any notes with the keyboard. At the end of a succession of notes, you can play the final note you sang to check the accuracy of your improvisation. Practice this exercise without any stable accompanying drones, chords, etc., forcing you to focus solely on horizontal interval relationships.

3.7) Melodic Improvisation

If you are comfortable improvising vertical and horizontal HSIs as in the previous two exercises, you can now practice singing improvised melodies. This exercise should typically be performed by singing solfège syllables, but you should also try melodic improvisation on scale degrees, horizontal HSIs, or vertical HSIs as related to the tonic. Try to create melodies that mimic musical styles that interest you. You may also push your stylistic boundaries by listening to melodies from unfamiliar styles and trying to improvise similar melodies, mimicking the melodic features of those styles. This exercise is creative, but do not sacrifice accuracy for creativity; occasionally check your pitch on a keyboard or other instrument to ensure that you have not deviated from the notes you intend to sing. Slowly increase the difficulty of your improvisations. Your melodies may initially stay in one key, but you should eventually try to add chromatic notes or fluidly modulate to other keys.

3.8) ACCOMPANIED IMPROVISATION

You may also sing improvised melodies while playing accompanying parts on the keyboard. Start by improvising sung solfège syllables over simple diatonic chord progressions. Challenge yourself further by improvising over non-diatonic chords, extended jazz chords, or modulating chord progressions. You can try improvising over chords in the left hand, bass notes in the left hand with chords in the right hand, a contrapuntal melody played in either hand, or any other texture you can imagine. While singing solfège syllables is most practical for this exercise, singing horiztonal HSIs or vertical HSIs above your tonic can also be effective. You may name vertical HSIs over the bass note of the chord (which is not always the root) or even try naming vertical HSIs of sung melody notes related to the top voices of chords. Feel free to change the feature you are vocalizing during your improvisation. You can choose any reference point or vocalization method you can think of for this exercise—be creative! Try to improvise passages that mimic specific genres, composers, improvisers, or pieces of music. This practice will expand your improvisation ability and your understanding of musical styles. You may skip this exercise if you do not have a suitable keyboard instrument; owning a keyboard instrument is not necessary to increase your musical fluency.

3.9) RANDOM NUMBER GENERATOR HSI SINGING

This exercise will use a random number generator to expand your ability to sing all eleven horizontal HSIs. Generate a list of numbers between -11 and 11 and sing successive horizontal HSIs according to the instructions. Generating random numbers will force you to sing HSIs you might not be comfortable with. The numbers generated might create successions of large leaps outside of your vocal range, but you may change the octave of any note for the convenience of your voice. You can use a smaller range (e.g., -3 to 3) if using all eleven HSIs is too difficult. You may "chase" each sung note with the keyboard, or avoid doing so for a greater challenge. Sing using the generated HSI numbers or solfège syllables.

Singing horizontal HSIs can be extremely difficult at first. As always, do not wait to master this exercise before working on other exercises. All the exercises in this book work together to improve your aural acuity. Practicing a little of each exercise will be more beneficial than extensive practice of only one exercise.

3.10) Vertical HSI Tracking, Sung

This exercise uses the tracking lines from the keyboard visualization exercises. This is exactly like the spoken vertical HSI tracking exercise, but every HSI will be sung. Start on your **seconds** line. Select a starting note and speak all possible vertical intervals on the white keys. For example, if you choose **Mi** as a starting note, your vertical HSI inventory for the white keys only is [0, 1, 3, 5, 7, 8, 10]. Play your starting note as a drone and sing through the vertical HSI inventory over the drone—you may ascend to the octave, then descend back down to your starting note. Once you have done that, hold your starting note as a drone and sing through your chosen tracking line, singing vertical HSI numbers above your drone. Immediately restart your tracking line and sing through it on solfège syllables over your drone; this will help connect the HSI numbers to solfège names and your mental keyboard. You may progressively try different starting notes and tracking lines containing larger intervals.

3.11) Horizontal HSI Tracking, Sung

You may also practice sung horizontal HSIs on your tracking lines. To do this, choose a tracking line and starting note, and sing horizontal HSIs on your tracking line. "Chase" your sung notes on a keyboard as you play; play the first note, hold it, and sing the second note. While singing the second note, play the second note on the keyboard, which should match the note you are singing, after which you can sing the third note, etc. "Chasing" your singing in this way will ensure that you are hearing the horizontal reference point of each sung HSI. If you sing a wrong note, i.e., a note that does not match the note you play on the keyboard, sing the correct note (the one you are playing on the keyboard) and continue through the line. When you have finished the line, immediately return to the beginning and sing using solfège syllables, still "chasing" each note you sing with the keyboard. Singing horizontal HSIs is often more difficult than singing vertical HSIs—this is normal and is not a sign that you are doing anything wrong.

3.12) SCALE VISUALIZATION, SUNG

This exercise will improve fluency in navigating different keys, helping you visualize all major and minor (natural, harmonic, and melodic) scales ascending and descending. Choose any scale and name vertical HSIs in that scale, all while visualizing the keyboard. Once you can visualize and name vertical HSIs, you should do the same thing but sing them, playing the tonic first on a keyboard for reference. After that, speak and visualize horizontal HSIs in each scale, then sing them. Once singing through scales on vertical and horizontal HSIs is comfortable, you may do the same on solfège syllables. Do not neglect any scale/key —you should be comfortable performing this exercise in all major and minor keys, clearly visualizing the respective white and black keys on the keyboard for each scale.

3.13) SCALE CONTEXT TRANSFORMATION

This exercise will help you understand the sounds of different scale degrees. While this exercise may initially feel torturous, it is one of the most valuable exercises for understanding the sounds of notes in different contexts. Pick any starting note, visualize it on the keyboard, and choose a key that contains that note. Speak solfège syllables ascending or descending by seconds from your chosen note through the scale to the tonic while visualizing the keyboard. If you choose the key where your starting note is tonic, just speak through the notes in the scale to a higher or lower tonic. After that, speak horizontal HSIs as you visualize moving up or down to the tonic. Do the same using vertical HSIs related to the tonic. For example, you can start on A in the key of D major and descend to tonic:

```
A descending to tonic in D major:

Solfège:              La   Sol   Fa   Mi   Re
Horizontal HSIs:      [0    2    1    2    2]
Vertical HSIs:        [7    5    4    2    0]
Scale-Degrees:         5    4    3    2    1
```

Once you have completed these spoken exercises, play the initial note you have selected on a keyboard (or another instrument), but *do not* play the tonic. Try to sing up or down by seconds through the scale, from your starting note to the tonic, using any of the above features (solfège, vertical HSIs, horizontal HSIs, or scale-degree numbers) without hearing the tonic beforehand. You can try to imagine the sound of the tonic, but avoid playing it on an instrument. If speaking and visualizing solfège syllables or HSIs in this exercise is easy, feel free to skip the speaking stage of this exercise and proceed straight to singing.

When you think you have successfully sung up or down to the tonic, play the tonic on a keyboard to check your work. Once you have done that, play your starting note again on the keyboard, but treat it as a different position in a different key. For instance, after performing the above example in D major, immediately sing A again and treat it as another scale degree in a different key; for example, treat the A as scale-degree three in the key of F# minor and perform the same exercise again, this time in the F# minor scale, singing down the scale until you arrive at your new tonic, singing on solfège syllables, horizontal HSIs, vertical HSIs, or scale degrees:

A descending to tonic in F# minor:

Solfège:	La	Sol	Fa
Horizontal HSIs:	[0	1	2]
Vertical HSIs:	[3	2	0]
Scale-Degrees:	3	2	1

Continue this exercise with the same starting note in many other keys and scale-degree contexts. If you are comfortable with this process, you may even start on notes outside of the scale; for example, you might start on A, treating it as #4 in the key of E♭. You might then move up to scale-degree five and ascend or descend through the scale to the tonic. You may not even need to play the tonic on an instrument to check if you did these exercises correctly—it is often apparent when you cannot sing your way back to tonic because the note of arrival will not sound/feel sufficiently stable. If this exercise is too challenging, you may check each note you sing as you ascend or descend to tonic and fix any errors you make.

Increased awareness of horizontal HSIs is helpful during this exercise. Because scales consist of a specific horizontal arrangement of half-step and whole-step relationships, and you are moving stepwise towards tonic, drawing your attention to horizontal HSI relationships can make it easier to force yourself into your target key. Horizontal HSIs often feel helpful because you lack the tonic as a reference point—the only reference point you hear is the first note and each subsequent note you sing. If you are having trouble with this exercise, I recommend singing horizontal HSI numbers very slowly to bring your attention to the half-step or whole-step relationships in the scale. The following example illustrates the same exercise moving through multiple keys, with horizontal HSIs from the starting note A.

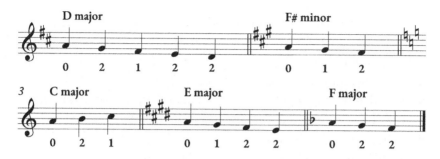

You can use a random number generator to force yourself to choose keys and contexts that may not immediately come to mind. For example, let 0=C, 1=C#, 2=D, etc., and generate a number 0 through 12 to pick a starting key. Generate a number between 1 and 4 to pick between major, natural minor, harmonic minor, or melodic minor. Finally, generate a number from 1 through 7 to pick a scale degree to start on and sing up or down to tonic. You may even generate numbers 1 through 11 to select chromatic starting notes within your key, with numbers indicating vertical HSIs over the tonic.

This exercise necessitates the ability to imagine a note in a specific musical context. Practicing this exercise will help you develop this ability. If you sing a note, it will inevitably have some associated musical context in your mind, even if you are not consciously aware of what this context is. When performing sight-singing tasks, you will rarely have an opportunity to hear the tonic to orient yourself—you must imagine the necessary harmonic or melodic scaffolding.

3.14) SINGLE-NOTE CONTEXT CREATION

Once you have achieved some success with the prior exercise, you can practice mentally shifting the context of a note *without* singing up or down to tonic. Because every note can have a multitude of contexts, it is possible to hear any single note with many imagined contexts. Sing any note and try to feel/hear it as being in a particular position in a scale. When you sing this note, *force* it to feel like it has a specific key context. For example, sing A (on the solfège syllable **La**), and force your sung note to feel like scale-degree five in D major. Then sing it again and make it feel like another scale degree in a different key, for example, scale-degree six in C# minor. Continue with any other scales that contain A. This exercise aims to help you understand how different scale degrees feel, improving your ability to change a single note's imagined key context on command. When you successfully imagine a note in a new context, that note should literally sound different to you. Obviously the pitch will not change, but the note will feel dissimilar because you have abstracted it from its prior context and put it into a new one.

If this exercise feels impossible, start by treating a note as the tonic and then treat the same note as scale-degree seven. Scale-degree seven is a good choice for comparison to tonic because it sounds comparatively very unstable—it should feel very different when imagining a note as scale-degree one versus seven. For example, sing the note A and imagine it as scale-degree one. The tonic is the imagined context most people generate when hearing one single isolated note. You may even sing a few scale degrees around this note (1-2-3-2-1) to help establish this note as feeling like the tonic. Next, sing the A again and try to force yourself to hear it as scale-degree seven in the key of B ♭ . If this is too difficult, you may play A and B ♭ on the keyboard or a B ♭ major chord to establish this new context. Notice how different these two contexts feel despite being the same pitch. Sing A again and switch your imagined context between these two keys; *choose* which context to hear this note in as you sing it, without adding any external aural support (i.e., without playing any other notes on a keyboard or other instrument). It can help to imagine moving a [1] up to B ♭ to force your sung A into the context of the B ♭ major scale. If imagining a contextualized note in this way is entirely too difficult, you should spend more time practicing the previous exercise.

3.15) ARPEGGIO SINGING

This exercise is an excellent way to internalize the sounds of chords. It can be challenging to hear chords by audiation because it is impossible to vocalize multiple notes simultaneously. You can circumvent this limitation by singing arpeggiated chords, i.e., singing through chords one chord tone at a time. This will make it easier to compress the sound of chords into a single verticality that you can hear in your mind.

Select any chord and pick one of its chord tones to start on. For example, you might select the chord A7 and the note C#. C# is the third of A7, so visualize C# and speak solfège syllables ascending or descending from C# through every chord tone in A7, visualizing each on the keyboard. Once you know what notes are in the chord, speak vertical HSI numbers on those notes, all related to the bass. If you ascend through chord tones, the bass will be the note you started on. If you descend, the bass will be the last chord tone you vocalize. Perform the same task using horizontal HSI numbers. Finally, play your starting note for reference and sing through all the same syllables. If speaking HSIs and solfège syllables is always easy, you may go straight into singing them.

You may also try to sing scale-degree numbers, especially if you are vocalizing a dominant seventh chord; in major keys, this chord only has one strictly diatonic context as the **V** chord (see Appendix C). If vocalizing a major or minor chord, you may choose a particular key context for it when vocalizing scale-degree numbers; for example, if you choose a D minor chord, you may treat it as functioning in any key in which that chord can occur, such as the ii chord in C major, the iii chord in B ♭ major, the vi chord in F major, or any of the locations in minor keys it would occur, and vocalize the scale degrees accordingly. For example, starting on C# in an A7 chord, treating scale-degrees as the members of the **V7** chord in the key of D:

Ascending:

Letter names:	C#	E	G	A
Solfège:	Do	Mi	Sol	La
Vertical HSI:	[0	3	6	8]
Horizontal HSI:	[0	3	3	2]
Scale-degrees:	7	2	4	5

```
Descending:
Letter names:   C#   A    G    E
Solfège:             Do   La   Sol  Mi
Vertical HSI:   [9   5    3    0]
Horizontal HSI:[0   4    2    3]
Scale-degrees:  7   5    4    2
```

In the descending example above, the vertical HSIs are named as related to the reference point of E because that would be the lowest note if you descend from C# through every chord tone in an A7 chord. Descending will generally be more difficult than ascending because you must imagine a bass note you have yet to hear. You should be able to perform this exercise starting on all chord tones of any chord. Fortunately, if you can perform this exercise on a particular type of chord starting on any chord tone, changing the root of the chord should present no problem—all chords of the same quality and inversion have the same horizontal and vertical interval relationships and will only differ in their solfège names.

When practicing this exercise, you may sing using whichever vocalization system is easiest—solfège, vertical HSI, horizontal HSI, or scale degree. However, it can be beneficial to intentionally find whichever system is the most difficult and attempt this exercise using that system. You may ease into singing chord tones by playing the bass note as a drone for vertical HSIs or chasing your horizontal HSIs on the piano. You may also perform this exercise on more complex harmonies or jazz chords for an extra challenge.

Do not feel intimidated if you do not know how to construct chords or if any music theory material mentioned is beyond your understanding. Appendix C contains information about chord construction, but if that material is too confusing, you may skip this exercise, do your best with other exercises, and return once you have learned about chord construction from another source.

3.16) INTERVAL COMPARISON

The interval comparison exercise is precisely what it sounds like. Play two different intervals on a keyboard and simply listen to them. Also, try playing one note on a keyboard while singing individual HSIs above and below the played note; try this with all eleven HSIs above and below the note you play on the keyboard. Try to take in any qualitative elements you hear, compare different HSIs, and describe how they sound alike and how they differ. Feel free to describe your experience using any terminology, metaphors, symbolism, etc. No description is too strange; for example, if you compare [1] and [7] and the [1] reminds you of the color of the lamp on your desk, that's fine. If you think [7] feels "glassy" and [1] feels "jittery," that's great! You do not need to explain why you have these associations; you are just trying to explore them, thereby gaining a better understanding of the feeling of each interval.

This exercise aims to help you discover how intervals feel different from one another, and your subjective perceptions of these differences are important because you will use these perceptions to differentiate interval sounds. The crucial part of this exercise is paying attention to how each interval feels. There is no concrete exercise task here—you are merely exploring your own unique perceptions. The most important requirement for differentiating and identifying interval sounds is persistence—keep practicing these exercises and you will eventually learn to differentiate all eleven HSIs.

3.17) FULL TRACKING PROTOCOL, SPOKEN AND SUNG

This exercise will combine all prior tracking line exercises to integrate your conception of vertical/horizontal HSIs, solfège syllables, and your visualized keyboard. First, choose a tracking line and starting note and speak through the entire line with solfège syllables. Next, do the same for horizontal HSIs, then vertical HSIs. Finally, sing through the same protocol in reverse order. However, there will be one change compared to prior versions of this exercise—only play the starting note on a keyboard (or another instrument) once; that is, avoid holding the starting note as a drone for vertical HSIs or "chasing" each note with the keyboard for horizontal HSIs as you had in prior versions of this exercise. To clarify this process, choose a tracking line, select a starting note, and perform the following protocol:

1. **Speak solfège syllables**
2. **Speak horizontal HSIs**
3. **Speak vertical HSIs**
4. **Play starting note once; sing vertical HSIs**
5. **Play starting note once; sing horizontal HSIs**
6. **Play starting note once; sing solfège syllables**

If you are feeling extremely confident, you need not play the starting note again for steps 5 and 6. Try to perform this exercise at progressively faster speeds and on tracking lines with increasingly larger intervals. Try performing this exercise on the 15-line tracking staff for an extra challenge.

3.18) 21-NOTE ROW, SUNG

This exercise is like the 21-note row exercise presented in Fundamental Skill #1, but you will sing each vocalized note instead of speaking it. You may sing each solfège syllable with or without naming accidentals, but make sure you are singing every note with the appropriate accidental while visualizing them on the keyboard. You can perform the spoken version of this exercise immediately before you attempt the sung version to ensure fluent identification of HSIs while singing. Do not attempt this exercise before you are very confident with the spoken 21-note row exercise. For an extra challenge, try to play only the first pitch on the keyboard for reference, only checking your accuracy at the end of the entire row. Maintain consistency of conventional interval numbers if possible.

A NOTE ON INTONATION

As you become more skilled at hearing and singing intervals, you may notice that some notes you sing may not precisely match the pitches of notes on the keyboard. For example, you may sing a [4] above **Do**, but when you check yourself on the keyboard by playing **Mi**, the note at the keyboard sounds slightly sharper than the pitch you sang. This discrepancy does not necessarily mean you were singing the interval incorrectly; in fact, you may have been producing the interval more accurately than your keyboard! Because modern keyboard instruments are tuned to equal temperament, the distance in pitch between each consecutive half-step on the keyboard is identical. This tuning is great for playing music in any key, but it results in intervals not tuned precisely accurately to the harmonic series above each fundamental pitch. In the simplest terms, the **Mi** above **Do** on the keyboard is not an acoustically precise [4] above **Do**.

When singing, you may produce pure intervals that are more in tune with the harmonic series above a particular note, and thus, your singing may be more in tune than the keyboard. Do not worry about this; your ability to match overtones above a note, i.e., to sing pure intervals, results from achieving a higher level of aural discrimination of pitch. You will eventually be able to sing "pure" intervals or intervals in equal temperament at will. Feel free to experiment with very slight changes in pitch—singing a pure interval above a given note may sound more pleasant or more precise than an equal-tempered interval despite not matching the pitch generated by a keyboard.

SYNTHESIS

THIS SECTION WILL GUIDE you toward fluency in the synthesis tasks: sight-singing and dictation. You may never need to engage in these tasks in "real life" musical situations, but your ability to successfully perform them is a good indicator of your overall musical ability, which will improve with your development of the three fundamental skills. I recommend much more sight-singing than dictation practice at first; even if you are more interested in developing your dictation/transcription ability, you should be able to read before you write.

Sight-singing and dictation require significant development of all three fundamental skills; however, it is not necessary to wait until you have achieved advanced fluency with all exercises in all three fundamental skills to attempt synthesis tasks. Feel free to attempt synthesis tasks concurrent with practicing the fundamental skills exercises. If synthesis tasks still feel nearly impossible, you may wait until you have progressed more with the fundamental skills exercises. Sight-singing and dictation require some development of all three fundamental skills, so these tasks may feel unbearably difficult if one or more fundamental skills are severely underdeveloped. In this case, you should spend more time on the exercises for whichever fundamental skill is the least developed. Think of synthesis tasks as a test of the development of the three fundamental skills. Even if you prefer focusing on fundamental skills exercises without attempting the synthesis tasks, you should occasionally attempt synthesis tasks to see how your fundamental skills have coalesced to improve your practical musical fluency.

You may eventually reach a point where you feel confident in synthesis tasks, especially sight singing. When the three fundamental skills are strong enough and sufficiently integrated, practicing sight-singing and dictation can help improve the fundamental skills themselves, so at that point, significant sight-singing and dictation practice is advised. Practicing synthesis tasks also helps you absorb common melodic phrases, idioms, and stylistic features from the music you are sight-singing or transcribing, so I recommend sight-singing and transcribing musical passages from styles in which you are most interested in achieving increased fluency.

You should continue to improve your performance for all fundamental skills exercises, even if your performance of synthesis tasks is adequate and improving without fundamental skills practice. You should constantly be trying to fill in the gaps you may have in any of the three fundamental skills, but I recommend simultaneously practicing sight-singing and dictation so the fundamental skills become associated with actual music. Developing the three fundamental skills is a targeted way to develop the abilities required for musical fluency, but musical fluency is best expressed through actual music.

Many musicians underestimate how fluent they need to be in the fundamental skills exercises for that fluency to transfer over into a synthesis task. Because each fundamental skill exercise is a relatively isolated task, the related skill may feel weaker when operating in the context of actual music. For example, you may be able to easily sing an isolated interval on demand in an exercise context; however, it may be much harder to sing the same interval in real time in a sight-singing exercise due to the increased complexity of the task.

SYNTHESIS: SIGHT SINGING

A) SINGING USING SOLFÈGE SYLLABLES

TO BEGIN SYNTHESIZING the three fundamental skills for sight-singing performance, choose a passage and attempt to sing it using solfège syllables while visualizing each note on your mental keyboard. If this is your first attempt at sight singing, find a rhythmically simple melody that moves mostly in seconds and contains no chromatic (i.e., out-of-key) notes. Even melodies that look easy may be very difficult to sing if you have little sight-singing experience. You may use any practice material you would like or try to locate some of the exercise compilations listed in the bibliography section of this book. Many of the exercises in these compilations are very difficult and include numerous clef changes, key changes, and rhythmic challenges. With practice, you can develop your sight-singing ability so that you can perform these exercises with ease.

You can play the tonic and the first note of the passage for reference before you begin, but you should work towards only needing to hear the first note for reference. If you continually lose your sense of key when first practicing sight singing, you may play the entire relevant scale or a simple chord progression in that key beforehand to establish the context of the passage you are trying to sing, though try to avoid this as much as possible—you should try to hear the musical context in your mind without it being provided to you. You may check your accuracy by playing notes on the keyboard, but do so as sparingly as possible and only when you are sure you sang a wrong note. Do not play the entire passage on an instrument and memorize it by ear; aural memorization is not sight singing.

B) ISOLATING PROBLEMS USING THE FEATURE STACKING PROTOCOL

If something goes wrong while singing a passage using solfège syllables, or if there is any hesitation, pause in the beat, or a note whose pitch accuracy you were not 100% confident in, you should break down the passage you are singing to expose any weaknesses. Your first attempts at sight singing will almost always require you to isolate problems and vocalize through different features. To do this, speak through the feature stacking protocol for your chosen passage:

1. **Rhythm**
2. **Solfège syllables**
3. **Scale degrees (if applicable)**
4. **Vertical HSIs (if applicable)**
5. **Horizontal HSIs**

If you experience any hesitation while performing any of the above features, work on that feature until you have achieved fluency. A poor performance when vocalizing any of the above features suggests a gap in your musical understanding of a melody. You may change the order of any of the above features, but it is usually best to vocalize rhythm first.

C) FEATURE STACKING, SUNG

Once you achieve spoken fluency, sing through the same passage using the following vocalization systems, visualizing the keyboard as always:

1. **Scale degrees (if applicable)**
2. **Vertical HSIs (if applicable)**
3. **Horizontal HSIs**
4. **Solfège syllables**

For some music, scale-degrees or vertical HSIs are less relevant. Music without a clear key may be difficult to parse in terms of scale degree; however, even in atonal music, you may find segments where you can temporarily determine the key, if only for three or four notes at a time. You can sing vertical HSIs related to the tonic for any unaccompanied melody that has a clear tonic, but you can only locate vertical HSIs that reference notes other than the tonic (e.g., bass notes) if your melody has a notated accompaniment (e.g., a piano accompaniment to the melody.)

Some music is practically impossible to parse via scale degrees but will still contain chords, temporary key centers, etc. You may forego singing scale degrees and focus on HSIs for music that lacks a clear key. Some music is so atonal that you may be unable to find any helpful vertical relationships at all. In such cases, start by singing horizontal HSIs and then move directly to solfège syllables; horizontal HSIs and solfège syllables are practical for any melody. Singing horizontal HSIs is especially valuable; if you can rapidly identify each horizontal HSI and you can fluently sing all eleven ascending and descending HSIs, you can sing through any challenging passage using your awareness of horizontal HSIs. Your understanding of HSIs will ultimately be absorbed into your vocalization of solfège syllables through your visualized keyboard, so you will eventually be aware of HSIs even when vocalizing solfège syllables.

You may play the first written note on the keyboard for reference before singing. Try to avoid playing the tonic, but you may do so if necessary. If you name a particular HSI correctly but continually sing the wrong pitch (e.g., singing a [3] when you should be singing a [4]), try to compare the pitch you sang with the correct pitch using exercises from the Fundamental Skill #3: Aural Identification section. For example, you might improvise [3]s and [4]s above and below various pitches, compare [3] and [4] using interval drills, etc.

FEATURE FLEXIBILITY

The aforementioned process is helpful to gain a thorough mastery of a sight-singing passage, but when practicing sight-singing more casually or if you are trying to quickly gain an aural understanding of a passage, you may sing whichever feature is most helpful at each moment. Consider the following melody that modulates from C major to G major:

You might start singing on scale degrees, switch to horizontal HSIs when chromatic notes occur, and then switch back to scale degrees once a new key has been established, as seen below:

If it is easier to think about the F# as a vertical HSI, you may sing vertical HSIs from the beginning, switching to scale degrees when the new key is established:

Singing vertical or horizontal HSIs is especially valuable if you need to "break out" of one key and into another. Major and minor scales are so ingrained in musicians' and music listeners' minds that singing an out-of-key note can be challenging. Horizontal or vertical HSIs are a great way to force yourself to sing such notes.

Singing on solfège syllables and switching to horizontal HSIs when necessary is an excellent way to sing through most melodies. Switching to horizontal HSIs can be very helpful when vocalizing part of a melody that contains chromatic notes. Following is the prior example melody starting on solfège syllables, switching to horizontal HSIs when a chromatic note occurs, and switching back to solfège syllables once the new key has been established:

Do   Si   Do   Re   [4]   [1]   Si   La   Sol   Fa   Sol

No matter what feature you sing, you should *be able to* sing all features. You should generally sing the features that are most obvious to you and would most assist your performance; however, you should also attempt to sing alternative features. Forcing yourself to use a reference point or feature that was not immediately apparent will improve your mastery of a passage. Strive to understand all note relationships in any musical passage, not only the most obvious ones. You should try to sing any melody upon first seeing it using solfège syllables; however, when this is too difficult, break the process down and try to make sense of the melody using scale-degrees and vertical/horizontal HSIs, eventually returning to solfège syllables once you have achieved a greater understanding of the melody.

Do not worry if you lack sufficient music theory expertise to confidently determine scale-degree numbers; skip them and try to sing HSIs and solfège syllables instead. While vertical HSIs tend to require a choice of which reference point might be the most relevant (e.g., naming vertical HSIs as related to the tonic, bass note, or chord root, etc.), horizontal HSIs require no such decision of any kind and only require the recognition of consecutive note-to-note relationships.

SYNTHESIS: DICTATION

DICTATION (SOMETIMES CALLED TRANSCRIPTION, transcription by ear, etc.) is the ability to hear music and notate it purely from hearing it. In a university class setting, this task usually involves an instructor playing a piece of music a few times, either recorded or at the piano. During this task, students with absolute pitch do very well, while the students without absolute pitch will generally experience a mild to severe sense of panic, write down an inaccurate transcription of what they heard, and only pass this test if the instructor is feeling generous. If the instructor is less generous, students with poor dictation abilities end up failing out of college music programs. Such a situation is obviously not ideal. As mentioned in the Theory section of this book, absolute pitch ability does not necessarily indicate general musical potential. Students without absolute pitch can become incredible musicians and should not be denied opportunities merely because they do not possess absolute pitch. With the development of the three fundamental skills and the proper framework for completing aural identification and labeling tasks, anyone can become skilled at dictation/transcription tasks. Every dictation task relies on success in the following three phases: Input, Identification, and Writing. Carrying out these phases in this order is essential to successfully complete a dictation task.

A) Input Phase

It is necessary to acquire a clear understanding of the music you are hearing before writing it down. If your mind cannot make sense of the music, there is no way you will be able to write it down. This circumstance seems evident in other areas: if you hear a sentence in a language you do not understand, it would be nearly impossible to accurately write it down because you cannot understand what you just heard. The input phase will help you mind make sense of the music; this is the most essential phase of dictation and should not be neglected.

The objective of the input phase is to sing the dictation melody after hearing it. If you can sing back the melody with 100% confidence, you have successfully completed the input stage. If the passage is too long or complicated to sing back all at once, try only singing back a tiny chunk, inputting a small amount at a time. Do not worry *at all* about identifying notes or writing anything down at this point—only try to reproduce it with your voice using a neutral syllable or vowel sound (e.g. "dah," "dee," "mah," "ah," etc.). Confidently singing a melody is the best way to test if you have understood the melody and if it has gotten into your memory. If you can confidently sing the melody faster or slower than the tempo you heard, that usually indicates a successful input phase. If you are in a situation where you are unable to sing out loud (a proctored dictation test, etc.), do your best to imagine the melody via audiation.

I recommend tapping the beat or conducting while listening to a passage and doing the same when trying to sing it back. Rhythm is an essential feature of music and can help you make sense of a melody when trying to hear and repeat it. You must keep track of the beat to understand each note's rhythmic position within the beat. Only consider the input task entirely successful if you can tap/conduct the beat while singing the melody. Do not try to listen to pitches and rhythms separately; listening to the entire melody as-is will help solidify your memory of it better than breaking it into smaller constituent features.

Most problems in dictation occur during the input phase. All other processes rely on the input phase, so a failure during that phase will prevent success at any other phase. Many musicians try to transcribe melodies without a clear mental conception of them—this never works. One way to practice the ability to sing back melodies during the input phase is to informally listen to melodies and attempt to sing them back, without ever trying to transcribe them. You can do this casually while listening to music, singing any randomly selected excerpt. You may also intentionally find increasingly complex melodies to listen to and sing.

The inability to reproduce a melody after hearing it can stem from many different shortcomings. This could be a limitation of your memory; a melody might just be too long to retain. If this happens, you may break the melody up into smaller chunks, proceeding through each dictation stage one small chunk at a time. Often, a problem during the input stage is one of comprehension rather than memory per se; that is, you may not be able to make musical sense of the melody, and your ability to discriminate the intervals you hear in the passage may be insufficient to sing it back. While labeling intervals or note names at the input stage is unnecessary, it can be challenging to sing back a melody if differences between intervals are not perceptually well-defined to you, especially if the melody contains chromaticism, modulation, etc.

Many melodies are in a single key; in these cases, you will likely make sense of the melody by hearing relationships between melody notes and the tonic. For these melodies, trying to identify and sing the tonic can be very helpful. It is much harder to absorb a melody into your memory if the location of the tonic is unclear. If you consistently have problems singing back melodies, I recommend spending more time on the exercises for Fundamental Skill #3: Aural Identification.

B) Identification Phase

Once you can sing a melody, you must identify its notes. The purpose of the identification phase is to accurately identify the notes in the melody and place them on your visualized keyboard—do not yet worry about the written notation. If you do not know what key you are in, feel free to pick any key to visualize on your mental keyboard. If you want to know the actual key of the melody and transcribe it in its actual key, sing the tonic or first note of the melody and check which note it is on a keyboard or other instrument.

You may aurally identify the notes you hear through whatever interval reference points are practical. If a melody is diatonic (i.e., all in a single key), it is often easiest to listen for each note's relationship to the tonic, conceptualizing the relationship as either scale degrees or vertical HSIs. If a melody is more complicated, listening for horizontal HSIs can be useful. Refrain from checking any notes on an instrument; the identification phase should not become a "guess and check" process. Slow down the melody's tempo when singing it back if possible—interval identification is often much more accessible at a slow tempo.

When first practicing the identification phase, you may hold a tonic drone on the keyboard and slowly sing through the melody, listening for scale degrees and vertical HSIs. Of course, to hold down a tonic drone, you must identify the tonic; try to sing the tonic (if applicable) whenever you work through the first two phases. You should ultimately not need to hold a drone or use an external pitch reference to this degree, but it can be helpful in the early stages until your interval identification abilities are more developed. Identify whatever notes you can and visualize playing the melody on your mental keyboard as clearly as possible, singing solfège syllables while visualizing. If you are having trouble with some notes, try to listen using a new reference point; this is often necessary if there are any chromatic notes in the melody. Horizontal HSIs can be especially helpful when trying to identify chromatic notes. You may also attempt to visualize the music notation as well as the notes on the keyboard, although keyboard visualization should usually come first.

You will eventually be able to hear a melody and immediately see it represented on your visualized keyboard. You can achieve this relatively quickly for simple diatonic melodies, but it will take much more time for melodies that contain larger melodic leaps or many chromatic notes. The better you are at the exercises for Fundamental Skill #3: Aural Identification, the more likely this spontaneous keyboard visualization will occur. If you can hear a melody and place its notes on your visualized keyboard with very little conscious thought, there is no need to go through intentional labeling tasks such as conscious identification of scale-degrees or HSIs.

C) Writing Phase

The writing phase is the final step in any dictation/transcription task and must occur after the prior two phases. Do not attempt to write anything you cannot sing and visualize on your mental keyboard. Mastering the writing phase may not be necessary for musical styles with less focus on Western music notation; absorbing musical ideas can happen even if you are only successful up through the identification phase, which still allows for the comprehension and reproduction of any passage without transforming it into notation.

To complete the writing phase, simply notate the notes you identified during the identification phase; this should be relatively easy if the identification phase was successful and your real-time music reading skill is adequately developed. Tap or conduct the beat while singing and visualizing the melody to ensure rhythmic accuracy for your transcription. If you are having trouble ascertaining the correct rhythms, try slowly tapping subdivisions of each beat while you vocalize the passage at a slow tempo. For more specific instructions for understanding subdivisions and rhythm notation, see the section on rhythm in Fundamental Skill #2: Real-Time Music Reading.

Once you have written down the melody, sight-sing what you have written and compare it to the melody you sang during the input phase. If there are any discrepancies between the two, make changes to your transcription and then compare them again. This comparison stage is the reason I recommend more sight singing than dictation practice at first; advanced sight-singing ability is a prerequisite for checking your work in a dictation/transcription task. For any melody you are transcribing, you may go through all three phases for small chunks of one measure (or less!) at a time, or you may complete each phase for the entirety of the passage you are transcribing. Selecting smaller chunks can be less frustrating, but you should attempt to transcribe the largest possible fragment of music in the shortest amount of time.

I recommend against using any system of "proto-notation," such as writing out the names of solfege syllables (i.e., writing "Do Fa Mi La" etc.) before writing actual notes on the staff, writing dots or lines of different lengths above the staff to represent rhythms, etc. These systems merely add another step through which you need to translate sounds into symbols.

If you are a musician whose primary focus is music that is mainly improvisational or less reliant on traditional Western music notation, such as jazz, blues, rock, etc., I recommend spending most of your time mastering the input and identification phases, as those may be most useful phases for these styles. If it is more practical for your musical goals, you may play the melody back on your instrument instead of notating it during the writing phase. Notating music is a valuable skill for most musicians, so I recommend gaining some ability to perform this task, but you should adjust your practice time in accordance with what is practical; you only need to practice the writing phase if it aligns with your musical goals.

HARMONIC DICTATION

The prior instructions are all targeted toward the transcription of melodies. You may also practice harmonic dictation, transcribing a bassline, chords, multiple independently moving voices, etc. Focus on only one voice (i.e., a single melodic line) at a time, and progressively add more voices upon each listening. You may go through the three phases for a single voice, then again for another voice, and so on. For multiple-voice dictation, it is usually best to start with the melody, followed by the bassline, and listen for any inner voices at the end. If the harmonies are evident from the melody and bass, it is sometimes possible to know how inner voices should proceed without hearing them. If you are listening for chords, try to hear the bass notes, chord qualities (major/minor, etc.), function in the key (i.e., Roman numerals), and then listen for vertical HSIs if applicable. You may skip the input stage when practical for harmonic dictation because some musical elements you might be listening for are not always singable in a straightforward way.

There is not one set method for hearing multiple voice dictations. The process for harmonic dictation will vary greatly depending on the characteristics of the music you are trying to transcribe. It may even be practical to listen for vertical HSIs before trying to transcribe any one voice. Your success at harmonic dictation will depend on your development of Fundamental Skill #3: Aural Identification.

INPUT AND IDENTIFICATION PRACTICE

One of the best ways to practice dictation is to work on the first two phases (input and identification) for any music you hear, without pausing or stopping the music and without worrying about writing anything down. You may sing the music back if necessary, but you will often be able to hear melodic fragments that you can quickly identify without needing to sing them first. You might even try to sing along using solfège syllables as you listen. Constantly listening for scale degrees or other interval relationships in any music you hear is a great way to practice that does not require sitting down for a practice session. Listen for any portion you can comprehend and try to identify and visualize it on your mental keyboard, choosing any key you would like if you do not know the actual key of the music. There is no need to be able to identify all the notes in any piece; just try to identify any chunk of notes whenever you can without writing anything down.

DEBUGGING

When experiencing failure during a synthesis task, try to pay attention to what part of your perception is failing and in what way. Doing this can directly address the weakest links in your musical fluency. For example, if you fail to rapidly recognize a note name when sight-singing a melody, that suggests more work on Keyboard Visualization and Real-time Music Reading exercises. If you are having trouble singing the correct pitch during a sight-singing task, take note of what interval was operative in your singing at that moment and focus on that interval by performing a suitable exercise in the Aural Identification section. If you constantly confuse the sound of a specific interval for another, work on an exercise that will compare those two intervals and try to solidify your conception of each.

FINAL THOUGHTS:
MOTIVATION,
PROGRESS, AND TALENT

YOUR PROGRESS IS ONLY LIMITED by your level of motivation, and your natural musical gifts (or lack thereof) need not have any bearing on your rate of progress. You can achieve the absolute highest levels of musical ability through the exercises outlined in this book, regardless of your musical background. Of course, this method will not instantly make you a master player of modern jazz, a brilliant composer, a great blues guitarist, etc. However, this method will give you the cognitive tools you need to accomplish your musical goals, whatever they may be.

When working through this method, you may sometimes feel like you are not improving; this will almost always be an illusion. As your musical ability improves, your expectations for yourself will also increase. These expectations will increase because the abilities you develop will feel progressively more natural, requiring minimal effort; however, because these abilities will feel so effortless, you will be increasingly less impressed with yourself for having developed them—they may feel so natural that you may not even realize there was a time when you did not have these abilities. It might be helpful to occasionally keep track of the limits of your abilities to keep yourself motivated; for example, if you come across a sight-singing passage that feels very difficult, keep track of it and come back to it in a few weeks to see how much easier it has become.

You may find the exercises incredibly difficult if you have no musical experience, but your progress may feel especially rapid because you are starting from scratch. This method is equally effective if you have decades of musical experience; it is never too late to profoundly change the way your mind understands music. While the exercises in this book may feel very challenging and frustrating, do not take this as a sign that you lack musical talent; rather, this indicates that you have much musical talent still to be developed.

APPENDIX A: CLEF REFERENCE

THERE ARE seven commonly used clefs based on three clef symbols: the G-clef, F-clef, and C-clef. The G-clef indicates where **Sol** (G above middle C) is located, the F-clef indicates where **Fa** (F below middle C) is located, and the C-clef indicates where **Do** (middle C) is located.

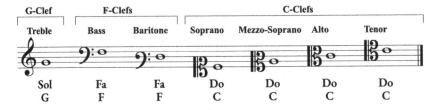

You may occasionally come across other clefs that function similarly to those above, but the seven clefs above are the only ones necessary to read any note in any position on the staff.

Appendix B: Major and Minor Scales/Keys

THE EXERCISES in this book will help you significantly improve your musical ability without requiring in-depth knowledge of music theory, but a basic understanding of major and minor scales and keys is essential because of their ubiquitous presence in music. I will present a cursory explanation of major and minor keys, but I recommend learning more about these topics from other sources.

Most pieces of music are "in" a particular **key**, meaning the notes in a piece will primarily be drawn from a limited inventory of notes. If a piece of music is "in C major," that piece of music will mainly use the seven notes in the key of C major, and most listeners will hear the note C, called the **tonic**, as a focal point in the music. A **C major scale** refers to the notes in the key of C major, played in order, ascending or descending. Many musicians will use the terms key and scale very loosely and interchangeably. Pieces of music can change key or **modulate** to a different key, changing the focal point and set of notes used. Many pieces of music use mostly **diatonic** notes, that is, notes strictly within the inventory of notes within a specific key, but many pieces will also use **chromatic** notes, notes that are not from the set of seven notes in one key. Chromatic notes do not necessarily change the listener's sense of key because they do not always change the listener's conception of tonic.

Major scales are constructed with a specific set of interval relationships. These relationships can be seen as a specific makeup of horizontal HSIs between each note or as vertical HSIs from the tonic. Because the notes in every major key have the same interval relationships with respect to the tonic, every major key will have the same vertical and horizontal HSIs but will contain different pitches, resulting in different solfège syllables or letter names for the notes in the key/scale. Every note in a key can be referred to by its **scale degree**, which is simply a number that indicates the position of a note within a scale/key.

Key/scale:	C major							
Letter names:	C	D	E	F	G	A	B	C
Scale-degrees:	1	2	3	4	5	6	7	1
Solfège syllables:	Do	Re	Mi	Fa	Sol	La	Si	Do
Horizontal HSIs:	[0	2	2	1	2	2	2	1]
Vertical HSIs:	[0	2	4	5	7	9	11	0]

Key/scale:	G major							
Letter names:	G	A	B	C	D	E	F#	G
Scale-degrees:	1	2	3	4	5	6	7	1
Solfège syllables:	Sol	La	Si	Do	Re	Mi	Fa	Sol
Horizontal HSIs:	[0	2	2	1	2	2	2	1]
Vertical HSIs:	[0	2	4	5	7	9	11	0]

Every major key will have one of every solfège syllable or letter name and a unique set of sharps or flats. This set of sharps or flats is indicated in music notation by a **key signature** to the right of the clef at the beginning of a piece of music. A key signature will "set" the piece of music in a particular key. The sharps or flats in any key signature will operate throughout the piece unless they are temporarily altered by an accidental placed on a note in those lines or spaces in the music notation.

Each major key shares a set of notes with a minor key whose tonic is the sixth degree of that major scale. This minor key is referred to as the relative minor of that major key; for example, **A** is the sixth note of **C major**, so the key of **A minor** will share the same notes as C major. Although the inventory of notes is the same in both keys, the aural focal point, and consequently the tonic for the key of A minor, will be A instead of C.

Music in minor keys often contains specific chromatic alterations on the sixth and seventh scale degrees. These scale degrees are often raised by one half-step; if the seventh scale degree is raised by one half-step, the resultant scale is called the **harmonic minor scale**. If the sixth *and* seventh scale degrees are both raised by one half-step, the resultant scale is called the **melodic minor scale**. If neither note is raised and the scale is played according to its key signature, the resultant scale is referred to as the **natural minor scale**. Regardless of these alterations, the key will still be referred to simply as "minor;" that is, there is no such thing as a "harmonic minor key" or "melodic minor key," only a harmonic or melodic minor scale. The alterations of the sixth and seventh scale degrees will be notated as accidentals in the music itself; they are not notated in the key signature. These altered scale degrees are flexible and will vary throughout pieces of music in minor keys. Feel free to look up additional information about minor scales and their altered versions; the explanation presented here is very rudimentary.

Key/scale:	A minor/A natural minor						
Letter names:	A	B	C	D	E	F	G	A
Scale-degrees:	1	2	3	4	5	6	7	1
Solfège syllables:	La	Si	Do	Re	Mi	Fa	Sol	La
Horizontal HSI:	[0	2	1	2	2	1	2	2]
Vertical HSIs:	[0	2	3	5	7	8	10	0]

Key/scale:	A minor/A harmonic minor						
Letter names:	A	B	C	D	E	F	G#	A
Scale-degrees:	1	2	3	4	5	6	7	1
Solfège syllables:	La	Si	Do	Re	Mi	Fa	Sol	La
Horizontal HSIs:	[0	2	1	2	2	1	3	1]
Vertical HSIs:	[0	2	3	5	7	8	11	0]

Key/scale:	A minor/A melodic minor							
Letter names:	A	B	C	D	E	F#	G#	A
Scale-degrees:	1	2	3	4	5	6	7	1
Solfège syllables:	La	Si	Do	Re	Mi	Fa	Sol	La
Horizontal HSIs:	[0	2	1	2	2	2	2	1]
Vertical HSIs:	[0	2	3	5	7	9	11	0]

Below is a diagram of all major and minor keys and their respective key signatures. The capital letter above each key signature indicates the major key that key signature represents, and the lowercase letter with the lowercase "m" indicates the minor key that key signature represents, i.e., the relative minor of each respective major key. The keys with seven sharps/flats are rarely used.

APPENDIX C: CHORDS

MOST MUSIC FEATURES both melody and harmony. You can think of melody as a prominent succession of notes that sticks out to the listener or the part you might "sing along with" when listening to music. In popular music, most songs are recognizable by the melody sung by a vocalist, though popular music does often feature instrumental solos with prominent melodies. You can think of harmony as the musical material that provides the background for melodies. Harmony usually consists of **chords**, which are collections of three or more notes. This section will present a cursory introduction to chords.

A chord is a collection of three or more notes in a specific arrangement. Chords are "**built in thirds**," meaning you can create a chord by stacking two or more notes in thirds above a bottom note. Chords with only three notes are referred to as **triads**. **Diatonic chords** consist only of notes from the key of the piece of music they are in. If you construct diatonic chords on each of the seven notes in a major scale, the chords will automatically assume certain qualities, either **major**, **minor**, or **diminished**, depending on their location in the key. Each chord quality has a unique arrangement of intervals between chord tones. Chords are also labeled with **Roman numerals** indicating which scale degree they are built upon; see below for a diagram of triads in the key of C major, with a table indicating which chords are major, minor, and diminished, with common chord symbols for each type of chord with the root of C.

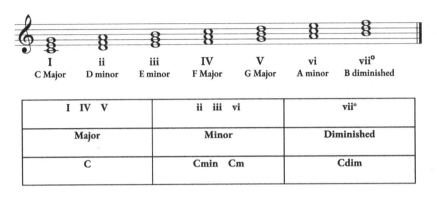

I	IV	V	ii	iii	vi	vii°
Major			Minor			Diminished
C			Cmin	Cm		Cdim

Uppercase Roman numerals indicate major chords, lowercase indicates minor chords, and lowercase with a ° symbol indicates diminished chords. These qualities are automatically established in any major key. In other words, you do not have to "make" a **vi** chord minor; it will automatically be minor if you stack thirds above the sixth scale degree. See below for a diagram of the chords in the key of E major; notice how the Roman numerals and chord qualities are the same as those of C major, but the roots of each chord conform to the notes in the E major scale:

Each note in a chord, or "**chord tone**," is referred to as either the **root**, **third**, or **fifth**. The scale degree the chord originates from is the root; the third is the first note stacked above the root, and the fifth is the note stacked above the third. For example, in a **C Major** chord, the **root is C**, the **third is E**, and the **fifth is G**. This chord will be called a C major chord regardless of the order in which these notes occur. The lowest chord tone present in a particular occurrence of a chord is referred to as the **bass**; this note may or may not be the root. If the root is in the bass (i.e., the root is the lowest note present), the chord is in **root position**. If the bass is a note other than the root, such as the third or fifth, the chord is said to be **inverted**.

Chords can also be constructed with four notes by stacking another third on top of the fifth; this fourth note is referred to as the **seventh**. These chords are referred to as **seventh chords**. Below is a diagram indicating the seven diatonic seventh chords in the key of E major:

The most common of these chords, the **dominant seventh chord**, is built on scale degree five. Below is a list of each diatonic four-note chord in major keys, with common symbols for each type of chord with the root of C.

I7 IV7	ii7 iii7 vi7	V7	vii°⁷
Major Seventh	Minor Seventh	Dominant Seventh	Half-diminished Seventh
Cmaj7 CM7 CMa7 CΔ	Cmin7 Cm7 C-7	C7	C°7 Cm7♭5 C-7♭5

The prior explanation is a very surface-level explanation of chords in major keys; there are many more chord types and chord symbols, but this should be sufficient to give you the knowledge required for all the exercises in this book that involve chords. There is also much variation in notational practices for chords, so you may see different symbols elsewhere. I encourage you to learn more about chords from external sources, applying any newfound knowledge to chord improvisation or visualization exercises.

APPENDIX D:
TRANSPOSITION

TRANSPOSING sight-singing passages into other keys on the fly is a great exercise, as it will force you to visualize the keyboard and read via interval relationships. Transposition is useful in practical situations if you are transposing a passage into a new key or trying to sing parts featuring transposing instruments. Singing parts with transposing instruments may not be practical for the style of music you play and may not be a necessary skill for all musicians; however, being able to read and sing a written part in any key is very useful for many musicians. You should eventually be able to transpose any musical passage into any key. Real-time transposition is a very advanced skill and requires significant development of the three fundamental skills and some knowledge of music theory, so feel free to ignore this section and come back to it later if you do not yet have a good understanding of key signatures, transposition, transposing instruments, etc. Knowledge of all seven commonly used clefs is necessary for this process; see Appendix A for an overview of these clefs.

A) THE TRANSPOSITION PROCESS

The most straightforward way to transpose a written part into a new key is to find the tonic of the written passage and imagine a new clef and key signature where you substitute the written tonic for a new tonic. For example, if a passage is in the key of C major and you wish to transpose it into E major, imagine a new clef where the written C becomes E in the new clef; if the part is written in treble clef, substitute a bass clef and imagine both this new clef and the new key signature of E major when singing the melody. Bass clef is used because a note in the third space in the treble clef is C, and we want to substitute the treble clef for one in which the note in the third space is E: bass clef. To sing in E ♭ major instead of E major, substitute the same clef, but imagine an E ♭ major key signature instead of an E major key signature. To treat this as an exercise, find a sight singing passage for which you could sing solfège syllables fluently and transpose it into a new key, singing new solfège syllables at the proper pitch for that new key, imagining whatever clef and key signature changes are necessary to transpose it into your new key. When transposing, all other features (scale-degree, vertical HSI, horizontal HSI) will remain the same; only the solfège syllables will change.

The following example in the key of F illustrates this process. Take note which line/space contains the tonic; in this case, F is in the first space on the staff:

To transpose this passage from the key of F to the key of G, for example, find the clef in which the location on the staff previously occupied by F would become G. In this case, G is in the first space on the staff in alto clef, so imagine an alto clef and the new key signature of G major, containing one sharp:

Sol (G)   Sol (G)

This results in the same interval relationships sounding at a new pitch level. Transposing to G ♭ is practically the same; just imagine a G ♭ key signature instead of G natural:

Sol (G♭)   Sol (G♭)

As always, while speaking or singing the solfège syllables, visualize the notes on the keyboard in their actual location while imagining the new clef and key signature. Try to perform this transposition task mentally without rewriting the passage with a new clef and key signature.

B) TRANSPOSING INSTRUMENTS

The transposition process can be more confusing for transposing instruments. Notes written for a transposing instrument sound at a different pitch than indicated on the staff. For example, on a B ♭ instrument, a written C will sound like B ♭ . Fluency with the three fundamental skills can make understanding the actual pitches of transposing instruments much more straightforward. This skill is useful for composers, conductors, arrangers, and jazz musicians working with common transposing brass and/or woodwind instruments such as clarinet, saxophone, or trumpet. To sing (and understand) parts for transposed instruments at their actual (i.e., "concert") pitches, you must imagine a new clef and key signature appropriate to the pitch of transposition.

To take an already transposed part and read it at its actual pitch, first switch the written clef for one that would make the written line/space on the staff containing **C/Do** become the pitch of transposition. For example, if you want to read/sing a part written in treble clef for Clarinet in B ♭ , find the clef where **Si/B ♭** would be on the line/space on

the staff currently occupied by C and imagine that new clef while read-
ing/singing. For a Clarinet in B ♭ written in treble clef, you will imagine
tenor clef—C is in the third space in treble clef, and B ♭ is in the third
space in tenor clef. In other words, switch the written clef out for one
where a C on the staff becomes the pitch of transposition, in this case,
B ♭ , and read/sing while imagining whatever clef makes that switch
possible. Substituting this new clef will get you the correct solfège syllables, but you will not yet have the correct key or accidentals. For this,
you will also need to change the key signature.

To determine the proper key signature to visualize, take the transposition pitch of the instrument, think about how many sharps or flats
that key has, and move that many places in the appropriate direction
around the circle of fifths—left for flats, right for sharps. You may also
think of this process as adding or subtracting sharps or flats. For example, on a B ♭ instrument, you will move two spaces to the left on the
circle of fifths from the written key signature, or add two flats to the key
signature because the key of B ♭ contains two flats. If you see a treble
clef part written for Clarinet in B ♭ with the key signature of E (four
sharps), move two spaces to the left from E on the circle of fifths,
arriving at a D key signature (two sharps); thus, you can read such a part
by imagining a tenor clef with a D key signature. Similarly, if a part is
written for Clarinet in A in treble clef, you would move three spaces to
the right on the circle of fifths from whatever the written key signature
is; you may also think of this as adding three sharps to the key signature.
Therefore, if the written key signature has zero sharps/flats for a transposed part for Clarinet in A, you would imagine an A key signature,
adding three sharps to the zero-sharp key signature, and a soprano clef
(**Do/C** on the bottom line, **La/A** in the third space) to read/sing a Clarinet in A at concert (i.e., actual) pitch.

If you are singing solfège syllables on a transposing instrument,
always sing the solfège syllables of the actual pitches (i.e., the syllables of
the pitches on the clef you are substituting/imagining), not the syllables
of the written notes on the transposed staff. You want to always
associate syllables with their actual places on your visualized keyboard.
Following is an illustration of the transposition process.

Take the following transposed passage written for Clarinet in B ♭ :

To transpose this into concert pitch (the actual pitches of the notes), you should first substitute the proper clef. The appropriate clef in this example is the tenor clef because we want to use the clef where the location of the note **Do/C** in the written clef (third space in treble clef) becomes the note of transposition, **Si/B** ♭ in the new clef (third space in tenor clef). You must also imagine a new key signature. The key of B ♭ contains two flats. Therefore, you should add two flats to the written key signature, resulting in a key signature with three flats and a tenor clef:

Keep in mind that the above concert pitch example is technically an octave lower than the actual pitches heard in the transposed passage; this should not be a significant practical problem, but you should be aware of the possibility of octave changes when transposing by clef. When sight singing with solfège syllables, you will very often be singing in an octave appropriate to your vocal range regardless of the written octave, so octave changes from clef transposition make little difference when sight singing.

Certain brass instruments are occasionally written without any key signature. In such cases, you should substitute a clef as usual and imagine the key of transposition as your key signature. For example, for a horn in F written in treble clef without a key signature, you should imagine a mezzo-soprano clef (**Do/C** on the second line on the staff) and an F key signature (1 flat). Accidentals will alter notes related to your imagined F key signature; in this example, a sharp before a note in the first space on the staff would indicate a B natural—raised a half step from the B ♭ on your imagined F key signature.

C) ACCIDENTALS

In addition to the above steps, you must be cognizant of any notated accidentals and how they would change the notated pitch when you imagine a new key signature and clef. There are ways to systematize changes in accidentals when transposing, but it is usually more practical to just keep in mind that the effect of accidentals may have changed; that is, it is easier to think about how the accidentals alter the notes on a case-by-case basis rather than trying to deal with a systematic large-scale mental reframing of all written accidentals. For example, a written sharp will generally raise a pitch but not necessarily be a "sharp note," and a written flat will generally lower it but not necessarily be a "flat note." A written natural symbol will raise or lower a note depending on its relationship to the key signature and prior accidentals. Exceptions to this exist with double-sharps and double-flats—a sharp occurring on a note after a double-sharp has occurred on that line/space in the same measure will comparatively lower a note, but these situations are not typical and would occur regardless of transposition. Pay special attention to natural symbols—note their effect on the written key signature and alter notes accordingly when reading/singing using your new key signature.

Appendix E: Exercise Reference

This section contains a list of all the exercises within this book and a very brief description of them, making it easier to find appropriate exercises during practice sessions.

Fundamental Skill #1: Keyboard Visualization

1.1) Individual Pitch Naming/Visualization, p. 50
Speak notes using solfège syllables and visualize on the keyboard.

1.2) White-Key Interval Cycles, p. 51
Speak solfège syllables ascending or descending a set interval from a starting note until you reach your starting note again. Always visualize on the keyboard.

1.3) Directed White-Key Tracking, p. 52
Have a partner direct you around your mental keyboard (up a 3rd, down a 4th, etc.). Speak the solfège syllable of the final note in the sequence.

1.4) Random Number Generator White-Key Tracking, p. 54
Generate a list of intervals between, at most, -7 and 7, and follow them

around your mental keyboard, speaking the solfège syllable of each note as you go.

1.5) Tracking Line Interval Identification, p. 55
Speak interval names (up a 2nd, down a 3rd, etc.) on tracking lines.

1.6) White-Key Tracking, Solfège Syllables, p. 58
Choose a tracking line and starting pitch. Speak the solfège syllables of every note on the tracking line while visualizing the keyboard.

1.7) 15-Line Tracking, Solfège Syllables, p. 60
Speak solfège syllables on a 15-line tracking line.

1.8) White-Key 7-Note Row, p. 63
Create a row of 7 random notes. Assign any clef and speak solfège names above and below a set interval from each note in the row.

1.9) HSI Cycles, p. 69
Speak solfège syllables, including accidentals, ascending or descending by a specific HSI from a starting note until you reach your starting note again. Always visualize on the keyboard.

1.10) Directed HSI Tracking, p. 70
Have a partner direct you around your mental keyboard using HSI numbers (up a [3], down a [7], etc.). Speak the solfège syllable of the final note in the sequence, including accidentals.

1.11) Random Number Generator HSI Tracking, p. 70
Generate a list of HSI intervals between, at most, -11 and 11. Follow the intervals around your mental keyboard, speaking the solfège syllable of each note as you go.

1.12) Vertical HSI Tracking, Spoken, p. 71
Choose a tracking line and starting pitch. Speak HSI numbers for every note on the tracking line as related to the starting pitch while visualizing the keyboard.

1.13) Horizontal HSI Tracking, Spoken, p. 72

Choose a tracking line and starting pitch. Speak HSI numbers for every note on the tracking line as related to each consecutive pitch while visualizing the keyboard.

1.14) Full Tracking Protocol, Spoken, p. 73

Choose a tracking line and starting pitch. Go through the entire line speaking solfège syllables first, followed by vertical HSIs, followed by horizontal HSIs. Finally, repeat the solfège syllables again.

1.15) HSI 7-Note Row, p. 74

Create a row of 7 random notes with no accidentals. Assign any clef and speak solfège names above and below a set HSI from each note in the row.

1.16) HSI 21-Note Row, p. 75

Create a row of 21 notes, with a sharp, flat, and natural iteration of each note. Assign any clef and speak solfège syllables above and below a fixed HSI from each note in the row. Name all accidentals.

1.17) Basic Scale Visualization, p. 78

Speak solfège syllables while ascending and descending through major or minor scales on your mental keyboard.

1.18) Tracking Lines in Key, p. 78

Choose a tracking line and starting pitch, and imagine a major or minor scale on the tracking line with its appropriate key signature. Go through the entire line speaking solfège syllables first, followed by vertical HSIs, followed by horizontal HSIs. Finally, repeat the solfège syllables again, all while visualizing the respective white/black keys for the selected scale.

1.19) Chord Visualization, p. 79

Select a chord quality, root, and inversion. Speak the solfège names, vertical HSIs, or horizontal HSIs of the selected chord.

1.20) Keyboard Improvisation, p. 80

Perform the following tasks on a piano/keyboard with your eyes closed: Improvise melodies with either hand while speaking solfège syllables. Play chords with either hand, speaking the solfège syllables for each chord tone.

FUNDAMENTAL SKILL #2: REAL-TIME MUSIC READING

2.1-2.7) Vocalized Feature Stacking, p. 89

Select a melody and vocalize it using the following vocalization systems:
2.1) Rhythm, p. 91
2.2) Solfège Syllables, p. 92
2.3) Scale Degrees (if applicable), p. 93
2.4) Vertical HSIs (if applicable), p. 94
2.5) Horizontal HSIs, p. 95
2.6) Jazz/Pop Chords (if applicable), p. 96
2.7) Miscellaneous Features (if applicable), p. 97

2.8) Polyphonic Solfège/HSI Vocalization, p. 99

Speak solfège syllables and/or vertical HSIs for every note in polyphonic music. Name notes in order from bottom to top, or speak the lowest voice first, followed by the highest voice, and then the inner voices.

2.9) Advanced Keyboard Improvisation, p. 104

Improvise a chord pattern in the left hand while improvising a melody in the right hand. Start with a simple left-hand accompaniment pattern and build up to a stride pattern in the left hand. Try this in all keys. This should be done with your eyes closed.

2.10) Keyboard Sight Reading, p. 105

Play music for piano or any other instrument at sight on the keyboard. Make sure you do not look down. Place a bed sheet or similar over your hands to avoid looking at the keyboard. Start with monophonic melodies using one hand at a time. For polyphonic music, play one part while vocalizing (speaking or singing) another part.

FUNDAMENTAL SKILL #3: AURAL IDENTIFICATION

3.1) Vertical Identification Over a Drone, p. 111
Hold a drone note and have a partner play notes above the drone. Limit the notes to the major scale in the key of the drone at first. Identify the notes being played via vertical HSIs, scale degrees, and/or solfège names.

3.2) Ploger Interval Drills, Harmonic Intervals, p. 113
Have a partner play a limited selection of harmonic intervals (i.e., both notes at once) on the keyboard. Speak the HSI name of the interval played. If you are incorrect, have your partner compare your guess with the interval that was originally played.

3.3) Interval Drills, Melodic Intervals, p. 117
Have a partner play a limited selection of melodic intervals (i.e., one note after the other) on the keyboard. Continue to hold the first note in each interval while playing the second note. Select only ascending or descending intervals for the intervals being compared. Speak the HSI name of the interval played. If you are incorrect, have your partner compare your guess with the interval that was originally played.

3.4) Interval Drills, Three or More Notes, p. 118
Same as 3.2 but playing more than two notes at once.

3.5) Vertical Improvisation Over a Drone, p. 119
Improvise sung vertical HSIs over a drone. Later, switch to solfège syllables.

3.6) Horizontal Improvisation, p. 120
Play a starting note. Improvise sung horizontal HSIs from each consecutive note. "Chase" each note by playing it on a keyboard. Forgo "chasing" each note for a more advanced version of this exercise.

3.7) Melodic Improvisation, p. 121
Improvise sung melodies on solfège syllables, scale degrees, or vertical/horizontal HSIs.

3.8) Accompanied Improvisation, p. 122

Play chord progressions, bass notes, contrapuntal melodies, etc., at the keyboard while improvising sung melodies using any syllable system for vocalization.

3.9) Random Number Generator HSI Singing, p. 122

Generate numbers, maximum -11 to 11. Play a starting note and sing horizontal HSIs from the starting note in accordance with your generated list.

3.10) Vertical HSI Tracking, Sung, p. 123

Choose a tracking line and starting note. Sing through vertical HSIs.

3.11) Horizontal HSI Tracking, Sung, p. 123

Choose a tracking line and starting note. Sing through horizontal HSIs.

3.12) Scale Visualization, Sung, p. 124

Sing through vertical HSIs, horizontal HSIs, and solfège syllables in all major and minor keys.

3.13) Scale Context Transformation, p. 124

Choose a starting note and a key that contains your starting note. Play that note on an instrument. Singing vertical HSIs, horizontal HSIs, or solfège syllables, ascend or descend by seconds to the tonic. Immediately sing your starting note again, choosing a new key, and sing through that key, moving up or down by seconds to the tonic. Only play your starting note as a reference—do not play the tonic before singing.

3.14) Single-Note Context Creation, p. 127

Sing a note and try to hear it as different scale degrees in different keys, without singing up or down towards tonic.

3.15) Arpeggio Singing, p. 128

Select a chord and one of its chord tones. Sing up or down from your starting chord tone through all chord tones using vertical HSIs, horizontal HSIs, and solfège syllables.

3.16) Interval Comparison, p. 131

Play a small selection of intervals back-to-back and compare the way they sound. Describe them in your own words.

3.17) Full Tracking Protocol, Spoken and Sung, p. 131

Select a tracking line and starting note. Perform the following protocol using each of the following vocalization systems:

1) Speak solfège syllables
2) Speak horizontal HSIs
3) Speak vertical HSIs
4) Play starting note once; sing vertical HSIs
5) Play starting note once; sing horizontal HSIs
6) Play starting note once; sing solfège syllables

3.18) 21-Note Row, Sung, p. 132

Create a row of 21 notes, with a sharp, flat, and natural iteration of each note. Assign any clef and sing solfège syllables, with or without naming accidentals, above and below a fixed HSI from each note in the row.

SYNTHESIS: SIGHT SINGING

a) Singing Using Solfège Syllables, p. 136

Attempt to sing a selected melody on solfège syllables while tapping or conducting the beat.

b) Isolating Problems Using the Feature Stacking Protocol, p. 137:

Speak through the following features for the selected melody until each is fluent:

1) Rhythm
2) Solfège Syllables
3) Scale Degrees (if applicable)
4) Vertical HSIs (if applicable)
5) Horizontal HSIs

c) Feature Stacking, Sung, p. 137:

Sing the melody using the following features.

1) Scale Degrees (if applicable)
2) Vertical HSIs (if applicable)
3) Horizontal HSIs
4) Solfège Syllables

Feature Flexibility, p. 139

Sing the melody while changing vocalization systems when practical; useful for quickly apprehending a melody.

SYNTHESIS: DICTATION

a) Input Phase, p. 142

Listen to the melody and sing it back using a neutral syllable. Tap or conduct the beat during all phases.

b) Identification Phase, p. 143

Identify each note using scale degrees, vertical HSIs, or horizontal HSIs.

Visualize the entire melody on the keyboard; check the tonic on a keyboard and visualize it in its actual key, or pick a random key in which to visualize the melody.

c) Writing Phase, p. 145
Notate the melody on staff paper. Sight-sing the written melody and compare it to the melody you sang during the input stage. Fix any discrepencies.

GLOSSARY

BELOW IS a list of selected music terms used in this book along with their definitions. The definition given here are coarse and do not necessarily capture all the nuance of each term, but these definitions are sufficient to describe these terms' usage in this book.

Accidental: Symbol applied to a note indicating an alteration of pitch, e.g., sharp, flat, natural, double-sharp, or double-flat.

Atonal: Music that lacks a focal pitch. Usually refers to music that does not adhere to major or minor keys.

Arpeggio: A chord that is rhythmically broken so each note is sounded individually.

Audiation: The act of imagining and understanding music in one's mind.

Chord: A collection of three or more notes that tend to be perceived as a cohesive vertical structure.

Chromatic: Refers to notes/chords that are outside of a key.

Clef: The symbol placed at the very beginning of a staff indicating which lines/spaces on the staff represent which notes.

Conventional Interval Number: The distance between two notes based on the distance between each solfège syllable or letter name.

Diatonic: Refers to notes/chords that are within a single key.

Harmonic Minor: A minor scale with the seventh scale-degree raised a half step.

HSI: "Half-Step Interval," refers to the number of half-steps between two notes. Music theorists sometimes call this number "pitch-class interval."

Key: A collection of notes around which a piece of music or segment thereof is based; is typically either major or minor.

Key Signature: A symbol placed near the beginning of a staff that contains accidentals. Usually indicates the key of a piece of music.

Melodic Minor: A minor scale with its sixth and seventh scale degrees each raised by a half step.

Modulate: Refers to the act of changing from one key to another.

Monophonic: Music consisting of one note at a time, or refers to an instrument only capable of producing one note at a time.

Natural Minor: A minor scale that adheres to its key signature, without alteration of the sixth or seventh scale degrees.

Pitch: How high or low a note is. Usually indicated by a letter name or solfège syllable.

Polyphonic: Music consisting of multiple notes occurring simultaneously, or refers to an instrument capable of producing multiple simultaneous notes.

Scale: A collection of notes played in ascending or descending order.

Scale Degree: The location of a note in a specific key.

Solfège: Refers to the seven solfège syllables or the act of reading music in general.

Staff: A set of lines and spaces upon which music notation is written.

Time Signature: Symbol consisting of two numbers arranged vertically on a staff. The top number indicates how many beats are in each measure and the bottom number indicates what type of note spans the length of one beat.

Tonal: Music based around a tonal center; usually refers to music that adheres to major or minor keys.

Tonic: The first note in a scale, i.e., scale-degree one. Can also refer to the chord built on this scale degree.

Triad: A chord consisting of only three different notes.

Bibliography and Exercise Compilations

Batiste, Édouard. *Petit Solfège, thèorique et pratique*. France: n.p., 1866.

Dannhauser, Adolpe. *Solfège des solfèges*. New York: G. Schirmer, 1891.

Fétis, François-Joseph. *36 Leçons de Solfège*. Belgium: Henry Lemoine, (n.d.).

Gédalge, André. *L'enseignement de la musique par l'éducation méthodique de l'oreille*. France: n.p., 1924.

Edlund, Lars. *Modus Novus*. Stockholm: Nordiska Musikforlaget, 1964.

Hindemith, Paul. *Elementary Training for Musicians*. London: Schott, 1974.

Lemoine, Henry, Adolphe Danhauser, Gustavo Carulli, and Albert Lavignac. *Solfège de solfèges*. Paris: Editions Henry Lemoine, 1910.

Ploger, Marianne. *The Ploger Method: Crafting a Fluent Musical Mind*. Nashville: Philagnosis Press, 2018.

Ratez, Emile Pierre. *Cent leçons progressives de solfège, changements des clés avec accompagnement de piano*. France: A. Leduc, 1908.

Starer, Robert. *Rhythmic Training*. Los Angeles: Universal Music Pub. Group, 1969.

ABOUT THE AUTHOR

Isador (Izzy) Miller is a music teacher with nearly two decades of experience teaching music. His interests in cognitive science, skill acquisition, and linguistics have led him to develop a groundbreaking method for improving musical ability. He studied with Ernesto Tamayo, Dr. Lindsey Reymore, and Marianne Ploger. He holds a bachelor's degree in linguistics and a master's in music theory, both from the University of Maryland. He lives in the Washington, D.C., metropolitan area.

Made in the USA
Monee, IL
27 April 2024

57602651R00114